The Next Chapter

CRYSTAL LYNN GARRETT

The Next Chapter

NAVIGATING LIFE & WEALTH IN RETIREMENT

Advantage | Books

Published by Advantage Books, Charleston, South Carolina.
An imprint of Advantage Media.

Printed in the United States of America.

10 9 8 7 6 5 4 3 2 1

ISBN: 978-1-64225-935-3 (Hardcover)
ISBN: 978-1-64225-934-6 (eBook)

Library of Congress Control Number: 2025911495

Book design by Megan Elger.

12-12-2025 2:49

To my incredible parents, Bill and Gayle,

Thank you for being the best parents a girl could ask for. Your unwavering love, guidance, and support have shaped me into the person I am today. You taught me the true meaning of love—not just in words but through your actions and the life you've built together.

Through your example, you've also shown me what retirement can be: a time to pursue interests, travel, enjoy family and friends, and spoil grandkids.

This book is a reflection of growing up a Hunt girl.
I am forever grateful.

With all my love,

Crystal

CONTENTS

ACKNOWLEDGMENTS

To Scott Tiras,

Thank you for being an extraordinary mentor and source of inspiration throughout my career. Your tenacious pursuit of excellence and unwavering commitment to clients set an example no one could rival.

Your guidance has provided me with countless opportunities to grow, learn, and push beyond my comfort zone. The lessons you've shared and the trust you've placed in me have shaped not only my professional path but also my ability to help hundreds of clients retire with confidence.

To my Uncle Richard,

Thank you for teaching me some of the most valuable lessons I've carried through life. When I was a young teen, you showed me how to think like an entrepreneur, work until long after everyone else has gone home, and count change without a register!

Your guidance gave me an early understanding of responsibility and the importance of thinking ahead. I am forever grateful for your wisdom, your example, and the foundation you helped me build.

To my boys, Magnus and Milam,

Thank you for your love, patience, and understanding as I pursued my passion for helping others navigate retirement. You both are my purpose for everything. You motivate me every day to be better—not just in my work but as your mother. This book is a reflection of the purpose that drives me, but nothing compares to the pride I feel in being your mom.

With all my love, M<3m

ABOUT THE AUTHOR

Crystal Lynn Garrett, APMA®, CFP®, is a nationally recognized financial advisor. With nearly three decades of experience guiding clients through retirement and beyond, Crystal is known for her clear-eyed, compassionate approach to financial planning—blending technical knowledge with a deep understanding of what matters most in life.

Crystal holds the CERTIFIED FINANCIAL PLANNER™ certification and is an Accredited Portfolio Management Advisor™. She works with high-net-worth families, executives, and individuals on everything from retirement income and estate strategies to charitable giving and long-term wealth planning.

Crystal has been recognized in many national rankings including one of AdvisorHub's Advisors to Watch (Over $1 Billion) in 2024. She was also honored among the Houston Business Journal's Women Who Mean Business in 2024. Her work and insights have been featured in Barron's, Bottom Line, and other national publications.

Passionate about empowering women through financial education, Crystal volunteers as a financial literacy instructor in Houston.

Crystal lives in Houston and in her free time, you can find her hiking, traveling, birdwatching, or behind a camera lens capturing the beauty of nature—hobbies that reflect her enduring passion for clarity, curiosity, and perspective.

INTRODUCTION

"Am I Really Ready to Retire?"

When Louise walked in, it was clear she was a ball of nerves. As she twisted her rings, shifting in her chair, I could see that the topic we'd met to discuss today was a stressful one for her. Louise had come to me via a referral from a longtime client to find out whether she was financially prepared to make the leap to retirement. Her friend had told her that she "had to talk to Crystal. She's either going to make you feel better or tell you the time isn't right." Louise wanted to know where she stood, but she was uneasy about the verdict.

Typically, when I'm doing this kind of assessment for someone, I have them fill out a worksheet that gives me a high-level view of their financial health. What is their current income, and how much of that do they spend and save? What kinds of cash or other assets do they have? What is their current cost of living? What are their hopes for retirement, and what kinds of changes do they anticipate in the way they spend their time (and money) when they leave the working world? She'd done her homework, and as I reviewed her answers, it quickly became evident that she was very well prepared financially for retirement.

As I walked her through the reasons I thought her assets were more than adequate to support her, I could see her relaxing—but just a little. She was so anxious about making this big life change that she'd gotten overwhelmed and almost couldn't absorb or accept that things were really going to be okay.

She peppered me with questions. "How should I choose to take my pension? What if the market goes down? How and when do I move money from my retirement accounts into checking?" All of these were queries I'd heard many times before and were easily addressed. I walked her through how it all would work. It wasn't until we'd gotten through her financial questions that some of her deeper concerns began to come to light. There was more on her mind than money—much more.

"But What Comes Next?"

When it came down to it, Louise's big question was this: What would she do with herself when going to work every day stopped being her routine? She liked her job. It gave structure and variety to her days. She valued the friendships she had with her colleagues, many of whom she'd known for years. If she were to retire and then discover she didn't enjoy having all that free time, she worried that her job wouldn't be there for her if she wanted to go back to it. Then what? Her family and friends were all assuming that she was ready for retirement. And while it was reassuring to hear that her finances were sound and she could afford it, this question still loomed: *"What am I going to do every day?"*

We talked through what her work role had been and the skills she'd developed in her career. She knew a lot, and I suggested there were multiple charitable organizations that would be grateful for that expertise. She brightened—she hadn't considered that but warmed to the idea of keeping busy and making new friends invested in a worthy cause. For some people I've worked with, tackling a big home improvement project can mitigate the impact of going cold turkey from the working world, as it demands their time and attention for several months. For others, a part-time job or work as a consultant can provide both engagement and extra cash flow.

If you're looking ahead to retirement, either soon or in the near future, you've probably felt these nagging concerns yourself. If you're no longer defined by your role at work, who are you? You're still interested in the world, you've got expertise and abilities honed by your years in your job, and you're comfortable with the give-and-take you enjoy with your friends at work. What will fulfill the need to feel relevant and engaged in life going forward—to be mentally active, to feel as though you can still make meaningful contributions?

This is unexplored country, and some of us had less-than-encouraging role models for retirement. Maybe you watched as your parents simply dwindled—took a new position on the sofa and spent their golden years watching daytime TV—and you don't want that to happen to you. But thanks to your work role, it's been a while since you were tasked with scheduling your own days, and you don't know where to begin. Like Louise, you're worried about what's beyond the horizon. It could be that your identity is so tied to your career that you're concerned your self-esteem will take a hit once you no longer have that hard-earned title to define you. Perhaps competition is so hardwired into your nature that you aren't sure what you can replace it with.

Here's the thing: *You're not alone.* Nearly every person I've worked with shares these concerns. Will they have enough money to retire on, and will they be able to find new routines and relationships to take the place of those they enjoyed at work as they navigate this new lifestyle? I get it; my work helping people build a fruitful and financially secure retirement for themselves is tremendously fulfilling, and I enjoy getting to know them.

There is a mass of contradictory information floating around out there from various pundits on the internet and in the media about how to plan for retirement, and that just adds to the confusion. Some of them address the money side, offering what they claim are hard-and-fast rules you need to follow to ensure your financial security. There are a million formulas put forth by a wide array of "experts" offering various "one size fits all" solutions. But, of course, retirement planning from the financial side isn't that simple, because everyone's situation is different. We each have our personal baseline for what we need to be comfortable and satisfied with our lifestyle along with individual dreams for our new lives that we want to pursue.

Good financial planning addresses your individual needs, assesses where you are in your preparation, and helps you to meet your goals. There's no cookie-cutter formula, and what works for you might not work for your buddy at work or your next-door neighbor, which is why we don't go to them for advice.

In the same way, good personal planning should help you to define for yourself what kinds of pastimes, hobbies, activities, or even a second career would enrich your retirement emotionally and spiritually, making your "second act" potentially even more satisfying and absorbing than your working years. Yes, there is life after retirement—and that life can be deeply engaging and full of discovery. But you've got to plan for it, just as you plan for your financial security, because it won't simply happen without your involvement and direction.

That's why I've written this book—to address these two widely misunderstood but interconnected pieces that are integral to your secure and satisfying retirement.

In the first part of this book, "Retirement in Black and White," I'll cover the nuts and bolts of solid financial planning, because no retirement can be happy if you're forced to cope with financial insecurity. We'll talk about how to assess what you've got against what you'll need, how to avoid the pitfalls created by poor planning, and how to avoid paying unnecessary taxes. Investment strategies often need to change when we retire, because how you invest during these years can either support your lifestyle or decimate it. And timing matters, maybe more than you know. When you choose to retire can impact taxes, for instance, though few people are aware of that. And are you inadvertently walking away from a bonus or stock options because of when you're planning to retire?

Should you go cold turkey, or are there compelling financial or personal reasons to ease into retirement via a part-time role in your current job or some other kind of business venture? For some of us, our retirement date comes sooner than we'd expected it, forced by a layoff or downsizing, and we have to reassess and rejigger our plans. The best time to think about something like that is well before it happens, because we all know that even the best-laid plans can be upended by unforeseen events, and security comes from having alternatives thought through ahead of time.

Not everything always goes according to plan, of course. Life occasionally throws us curveballs, but there are strategies to mitigate the financial impact those unhappy surprises can have, and we'll talk about those too.

Do you want to leave a legacy to your family or to a charity or cause you're passionate about? There are multiple ways to plan for these bequests, and how you choose to arrange them can help you pass along your wealth without creating tax burdens or other problems for the ones you leave it to.

In the second part of the book, "Retirement in Color," I'll address the "soft skills" you'll need to get the most out of your second act. Where can you find social connection, and how can you develop or discover new interests and skills?

What gives meaning and purpose to your life now, and how can you dig deeper into those satisfying pursuits in retirement?

If you're in a marriage or long-term relationship, retirement will impact that, too, and both you and your partner will need to adjust to all this new together time. Who will you spend time with, and how will you plan your days?

Are you considering downsizing or possibly splitting your time between two households in different areas? Many people assume that downsizing will help them stretch their financial resources further, but that's often not the case. I'll discuss when a move makes sense and when it might not, and how to safely try out a new location without making a life-changing leap.

Other kinds of changes can and do happen in life. An unexpected illness or the loss of a spouse or partner can upend our lives. Sometimes a long-term relationship ends when one or the other partner outgrows it or just wants out. Any of these kinds of events are life changing, and it's important again to think ahead of time about how we'll be impacted and how best to cope.

I'd be willing to bet that no matter how knowledgeable you are, you'll discover something new to consider in every chapter in this book—but feel free to dip into chapters that speak to the questions you have right now. My feeling is that the more you know and the sooner you know it, the better you can do when it comes to crafting your best retirement.

My clients are all smart people. Most have done well in their working lives and look forward to a rewarding retirement. They've done their homework and are all in when it comes to preparation. They come to me because over the last twenty-nine years, I've already retired about 250 times, in that I've gone through the preparation process with at least that many people—advising them, helping them to prepare, and getting them safely past the pitfalls that this change of lifestyle can present. It's rewarding work, knowing I'm steering them toward the security they need to go confidently into this great new phase of their lives, when they can enjoy the fruits of their labors and pursue what makes them happy.

Remember, retirement is a journey, not a destination, so pack accordingly! I'm confident that this book will help you to map out a safe route to the retirement you've dreamed of.

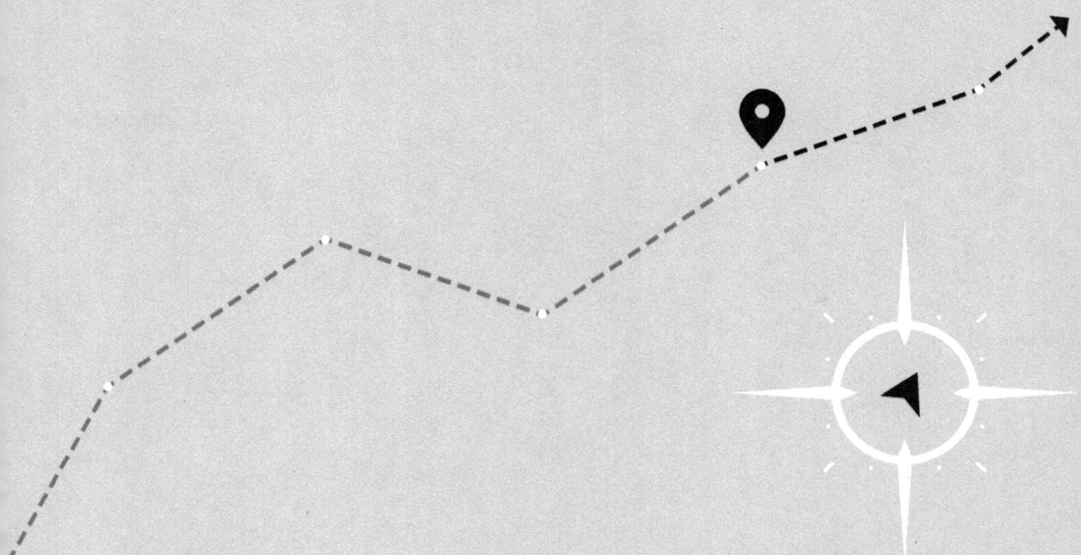

PART I

Retirement in Black and White

In part I, I'll tackle the financial side of retirement—everything you need to know about money and how your finances will work in this new phase of your life. This is where most people start when they begin their retirement planning, so we'll address this first.

CHAPTER 1

"Do I Have Enough Money to Retire?"

> *"How much do I have?"*
>
> *"How much do I need to retire?"*
>
> *"What if I don't have enough?*

These are the three questions I hear most often in my initial meetings with new clients—and understandably so. There's so much information and misinformation in circulation regarding what constitutes "enough" and how to measure what you've saved against that standard. But "enough" looks different to each of us, so it's clearly not a one-size-fits-all situation.

First, Where Does It Go?

Knowing what you've got in income and where it goes every month is key to planning, so start there. Begin with a budget, because if you don't know what you're spending on a regular basis, you can't assess what you're going to need. When I use the word *budget* in these conversations, I sometimes see the client's face fall—but honestly, it's not about passing judgment on how you choose to spend your money. If you routinely spend fifty dollars a week or more on steaks or wine or both, that's fine—as long as you know where it's going. A budget just lets us know what you spend maintaining the lifestyle you enjoy now, because most of us don't want to downgrade to a less comfortable lifestyle than we currently enjoy. Some folks assume they're going to spend less in retirement, but at the end of the day, chances are you're not changing your stripes just because you're retired. You're still going to eat out at the same restaurants; you're still going to hang out with the same friends and play at the same golf course and shop at the same places as you do now. Your taste in cars won't change, and your electric bill won't either.

That's why we need to drill down on how much you spend every month, because if we're assuming you need $8,000 a month and it turns out you really need $12,000, and we've used that erroneous figure to decide whether you can safely retire from your job, that's bad. I certainly don't want to have to make the call saying you need to go back to work, and you don't want to get it.

Another way to approach this is by looking at your net paychecks. If your take-home pay is $6,000 per month, are you regularly spending all of that? If so, then you'll probably need $6,000 a month coming in. We need to look at what may be included with your pay that we'll have to replace once you've retired. Medical insurance is often one of those gaps that need to be filled. Your tax situation may change too.

Did you receive an annual bonus? That may have been what you set aside to purchase a new car every three years, or it may have been used to pay taxes, so we need to address what impact losing that bonus will make on your income in retirement.

Occasionally I meet with someone who's absolutely on top of this and knows where every penny goes. That kind of granular view is the exception, though. Most people run on autopilot, apart from emergencies, and as long as they're in the black at the end of the month, they don't look much further.

A really useful tool in figuring out where your money goes is your credit card statement. As the use of checks has become less common, most of us pay bills and make purchases using our credit cards. That gives us a simple way of looking at both your recurring and exceptional purchases to accurately track spending.

"But I Can Cut Down!"

When I hear this, I push back on people to be realistic, because we all know that behaviors don't just change overnight. Unless you've taken steps well before retirement to modify how you spend and gotten comfortable with it, chances are good that you won't be as effective at cutting back as you imagine. Why set yourself up to fail? Again, you don't want to be the person getting that "time to go back to work" call from your wealth manager.

That said, there are some expenses that *can* disappear when you've retired. If you're in the twentieth year of a thirty-year mortgage, it's going to be paid off soon, so that's money that can go elsewhere. If you've got adult kids who are still dependent on you for some of their support, we can assume that your cash won't always be needed to finance their tuition, groceries, or even their cell phone plan. In the meanwhile, though, we need to factor those costs in.

Sometimes expenses just come out of left field. A client of mine, Janet, had a very talented son who wanted to sing classical music, and she and her husband worked longer than they would otherwise have had to, to finance his training abroad. But his voice just didn't develop as he'd hoped, and the more he saw of life as a third-string musician, the less interested he was in joining their ranks. Unable to get work outside of chorus jobs with small regional opera companies, he ended up going back to school to get a culinary degree—and now his parents are financing that too. That threw a wrench into their retirement plans, and Janet was forced to make the tough choice to go back to work.

I've noticed that my wealthiest clients are the childless ones and that the folks who struggle the most with keeping a lid on these kinds of expenses are the ones who never learned to tell their kids no.

We'll need to factor in your debts, too, and price servicing them into your retirement. Outstanding loans, credit card debt, and other debt are part of your monthly costs until they're paid off. Credit card debt in particular can be a real budget killer, and if you've strayed into high-interest territory by failing to pay off your balance every month, you need to get a handle on that now, not later. If it means cutting back on some planned-for treats or trips, that's okay, because credit card rates currently verge on the extortionate. What you don't want is a debt bomb aimed at your nest egg and gathering speed and size as it approaches.

That said, I don't worry too much about a mortgage near its end point or a low-interest car loan. These are predictable fixed expenses that have an end-by date.

How Do You Picture Your Dream Retirement?

That's an important factor as we quantify how much is enough. Maybe you love to travel and have been waiting to cut loose and see the world. I've got clients in their mid to late eighties who are still out taking cruises and going on tours. For most of us, our traveling days gear down in our eighties and we don't need to budget those expenses into our calculations past that point—but this couple intends to keep going until they can't.

You can see why it's difficult to make hard-and-fast judgments about how much money is going to be enough to finance your retirement. Your future health and length of life play important roles too, of course, but they're impossible to predict. As I tell my clients, if you could tell me when you're going to die, my job would be a whole lot easier! If that were the case, we'd know exactly how much you could afford to spend, what your level of risk tolerance was, and all the rest. Fortunately—in my opinion, anyway—we don't have that information, so the prudent thing is to plan for a long life.

"Where Will My Income Come From?"

What will your postretirement income consist of? You may have pensions coming to you and will be taking Social Security at some point. Other sources of income might include the rent on investment properties, payments from annuities, individual retirement accounts

(IRAs), and qualified employer-sponsored retirement plans (QRPs) including 401(k), 403(b), and governmental 457(b).

When you start to draw on your retirement accounts is mandated by the government. As of this writing, the latest an individual can start taking required minimum distributions (RMDs) is age seventy-five.

We'll also want to talk about growing that nest egg. Often people getting ready to retire assume that what they have at that point is the apex of their wealth and that the future will be about drawing it down, but that shouldn't be the case.

The $1 Million Rule of Thumb

If you've been putting away money throughout your working life, you're looking at that nest egg now and wondering how to factor it into your postretirement income. Here's a simple formula I share with my clients to help them get a handle on what they can prudently plan on: the $1 million rule of thumb, which tells us that for every $4,000 you need above and beyond your fixed postretirement income, you'll need $1 million in the bank to replace it.

This formula is based on payout rates, but it does provide some quick context for you. If you tell me that you require $10,000 a month, you will need $2.5 million in retirement assets to generate that, setting aside whatever other income streams you've got. You'll still have to pay taxes on it, but we can get a good ballpark figure with this formula, certainly enough to show us if we're in the game or way off.

Once we can see that, we can drill down a little bit further to see how close we are. Do we need to run formal projections? If by our calculations we discover you can afford to spend $12,000 a month, but you're only spending $8,000, we're in good shape. On the other hand, if you can afford to spend $10,000, and you're spending $9,000, that's a little tighter, but assuming your mortgage is going to be paid off, that will give us a little more breathing room. That $1 million rule of thumb is really helpful for us in those initial meetings when we're talking about retirement and how much we have to do to get us where we need to be.

In my experience, I'd say about 50 percent of my new clients arrive not really having figured this out. The other half are pretty clear on where they stand but want an expert opinion and some strategies to help them get the most out of what they have. Many times, I've been able to tell a client in their fifties that they're already where they need to be if they want to retire early, and that's always a pleasant surprise. It's much rarer to have to explain to a client that even though they're ready to retire, their finances won't allow them to do so quite yet.

Most often, my clients come in well ahead of retirement, and we talk about their plans and their timetable. I can tell them whether they're on track and, or if they're not, what we can do to get them there. That perspective is so important, because it empowers you to make smarter choices now that will benefit you for the rest of your life.

"I'm Not Sure I'm Ready to Retire"

Like Louise, you may be uneasy about how you'll fill your days after retirement. Many of us lacked healthy role models growing up when it came to retiree life, and you may not relish the idea of taking up a "new position"—on the couch. That's not what today's active retirement looks like from my perspective; we're mostly staying healthier longer and are able to enjoy a more vigorous and longer retirement than our parents or grandparents. But it's a common worry, especially among those who've enjoyed their working years and are invested in their careers—or who may want/need more money coming in to cover financial shortfalls.

The good news is that you don't have to go cold turkey! Retirement doesn't have to be all or nothing.

A classic example is a schoolteacher who leaves the regular workforce but continues to teach when they wish to, as a substitute. Alternatively, I've seen teachers start consulting companies to do professional development seminars for other teachers as well as take up tutoring, where you can really make your own schedule. Some former teachers work grading SAT tests. Sometimes a teacher will move from the public sector, where the benefits are better, to work in a private school where they're offered more flexibility.

An attorney may decide to cut their caseload in half or take up consulting work in their specialty. Some do mediations, which allows them the flexibility to look at their calendar and decide when they want to work and how many cases they want to take on. CPAs and engineers can do the same kinds of things in their areas of expertise. Many companies don't want or need full-time or long-term employees in these kinds of jobs and are delighted to work with independent contractors.

One of my clients was a pediatrician who really loved his work but wanted more downtime and flexibility. When he sold his practice, he was able to negotiate a part-time position working with the new doctor/owner. Another physician had had enough of the hands-on work of his profession and started up a consulting business, working with hospitals.

If you do decide to start your own business, you'll want to consider the legal and tax ramifications of that and possibly create an LLC organization.

I have so many clients who have already put a lot of thought and dreams into the "What will I do?" question, and they're raring to go. They've got trips planned. They're babysitting their grandchildren three days a week. Some of them are building their retirement dream homes or taking on big projects in their current homes.

The fact is, for most people life stays busy after retirement. What I hear most often is "I don't know how I ever had time to work!" The 10 percent who aren't happy—who "fail" retirement—are those who haven't put any thought into creating a vision for the years ahead. I encourage you to include thinking into your future as you plan for retirement—and I'll talk more about that in the second part of this book.

Remember, retirement isn't just about when you *have* enough; it's also about when you've *had* enough. You'll know when that happens, and sometimes just the knowledge that, yes, you can afford to leave your job and explore your other interests is enough to make you start looking a little more critically at your work.

Maybe there's a new project coming up and you're going to get a new boss, and it hits you that you don't relish the idea of going through another one of these transitions. Maybe there's another new operating system you'll have to learn or another layer of complications you'll be tasked with dealing with, and you realize you've had enough.

If that date comes earlier than you had imagined it would, the great news is that if your finances are in order, you'll have more years to enjoy yourself and pursue new interests.

Action Plan

- Take inventory of your assets and liabilities (debts).
- Calculate how much you spend monthly.

- Calculate what you need to have, using the $1 million rule of thumb.
- Remember that you have options, no matter where you're at!

CHAPTER 2

Taxes and Retirement

> *"Will my tax situation change after retirement?"*
>
> *"What new taxes and rules should I be aware of?"*
>
> *"What can I expect from Social Security?"*

So many things change in your retirement, and that holds true for your taxes too. Nobody loves paying taxes, and arguably the only thing worse than paying what you owe is paying more than you should have because you've inadvertently stepped on a tax land mine you could have avoided if you'd known the rules.

Let me begin this very important chapter with a caveat: Tax laws change often, both at the state and federal levels, and keeping up with the changes is a full-time job for professional tax preparers and CPAs who specialize in this area. It's not a great idea to cut corners when it comes to tax preparation and planning, because what might seem like a bargain when you choose it can wind up being a very expensive lesson down the road about the folly of doing it yourself—like some folks I met: Brad and Mary.

Brad and Mary had been very pleased with themselves when they decided they didn't have to touch their 401(k)s or lump-sum pensions, because they'd figured they had enough to live on between cash they'd saved and Mary's severance package. Thinking it would be better to defer touching the 401(k) retirement plan for as long as possible, they were grateful for the severance and lived on it for several years. But what they didn't see coming was the price of a new car later on. When their car died on them, they had to pull a big lump sum out of Brad's 401(k)—$50,000 in order to cover the cost of the car and the big tax bite they now owed on that money. Even with the trade-in, they needed to take $50,000 just to net the $35,000 they needed.

And that wasn't even the worst part.

The worst part was that taking that big a sum put them into a higher tax bracket than they had been in, so they were paying more in taxes on all their money than previously. It turned out that their careful planning had led them to a tax land mine. But it's one they would have stepped on sooner or later, because once you spend down your already-taxed cash assets (like a severance), you're down to having to depend on your pretax retirement accounts to make up whatever shortfall there is in your income. Now you have zero control over your tax bracket, and that's not good.

In this chapter I'm going to address some of the most common mistakes we see people make around taxes and the strategies we use with our clients to mitigate or avoid those pitfalls.

I'll be talking about the following:

- Tax leveling
- Tax diversification
- Tax-loss harvesting
- Roth conversions

- Required minimum distributions
- How moving can change your taxes
- Qualified charitable distributions
- Donor-advised funds

Using Tax Leveling to Protect Your Savings

We feel great about retirement when we've done a good job saving up and putting together the assets to support our postemployment loves. But *how* we save matters too. I tell my clients who are preparing for retirement that they need to have more in place than just those workplace retirement accounts and IRAs. They also want to build non-IRA retirement for tax diversification, or they will wind up paying more than they want to in taxes. How?

Let's say you need $5,000 a month to cover expenses. If you're taking that money out of your 401(k) plan, you will actually need to withdraw $6,500 or $7,000 a month to wind up with that $5,000, because you've got to pay taxes on it. So, you pull out that $6,500, and $1,500 of it goes to the IRS. And like Brad and Mary, you may find yourself thrust into a higher tax bracket to boot.

If you've got a mix of pre- and after-tax accounts, you're in a better position if you need a new car or other lump-sum expenses. And what if income tax brackets change? Historically, federal income tax brackets have been as high as 90 percent! With money in those after-tax accounts, if you need a big lump sum for whatever reason, you can take less of it from those pretax accounts that impact your bracket and more from your nontaxable accounts. It puts you in control. We call this *tax leveling*.

In using tax leveling, I go into a client's account every year to see how they're doing. How much income do they have? How much more do they need if their income isn't sufficient to meet their expenses? From what sources can we pull that additional income? If they're in the 12 percent bracket, for instance, we might be able to pull more than they need and still keep them in that relatively low tax bracket.

Say the client's living expenses per month come to $5,000. If they have $20,000 in Social Security income, they'll have to pay taxes on 85 percent of it. We will take another $3,000 from retirement accounts to supplement that. The 12 percent bracket goes all the way up to about $90,000, so we haven't gotten close to that mark. We need to be sure there's no other income we're overlooking, like interest and ordinary dividends, because those count against the tax bracket. I might suggest the client could take an additional $10,000 without changing brackets, not because the client needs it but because it gives us the opportunity to move that money over to a Roth IRA.

Tax Diversification

We see many clients who have done a stellar job saving for retirement. They come in with more than what they need set aside in workplace retirement plans, pensions, and 401(k)s. Even so, though they've done a good job saving, they can unintentionally put themselves in a tight spot because of their failure to manage their tax bracket.

One thing history shows us is that tax brackets *do* change, and if you have all your money in pretax accounts, you have no ability to control your taxable income during retirement. That means you'll be stuck with whatever those top tax rates are unless you spend less money.

To avoid that scenario, as you prepare for retirement, maintain some non-IRA balances. Don't spend those down first; you want those already-taxed accounts in place to help you to control your tax bracket. And you need to be wary of Roth conversions, because it's easy to make mistakes. People assume they're better off taking dollars out of their pretax IRAs and investing them into Roths, where they will grow tax-free. But they often neglect to consider the amount of tax they'll have to pay in order to do that. There's a break-even period to consider. How long does it take you to make up for all that tax you paid to take the money out? Don't forget that in retirement, your Medicare premiums are based on your income from the two years prior, which means that in addition to the taxes you're paying, you're going to see your Medicare premium bumped up two years later in what is essentially a surtax. I call this "collateral damage" on a Roth conversion, so if you're considering this move, talk first to your wealth management professional about the impact this might have on your taxes going forward.

Tax-Loss Harvesting

Even bad or uncertain times in the stock market can present opportunities for the investor who's had a loss. To be frank, a lot of wealth managers may not take advantage of tax-loss harvesting and don't explain it to their clients. Some are afraid of pointing out the losses to clients. But often it's absolutely the right thing to do. We think it's a valuable tool because it's not just about your rate of return while you're invested or even saving up for retirement; it's about how much of that money you get to keep. Here's how it works.

Let's say, as was the case for most people in 2022, your stock portfolio had a rough ride. You likely had some holdings that went down significantly, because there were very few places to hide in that market. If you had something that was worth $10,000 on January 1, it was probably worth less—maybe much less—a few months later. But it's not all loss, because tax-loss harvesting can help you when your position is down in value by selling off at a loss and claiming the benefits associated with that loss. And this works in after-tax accounts, whether we're talking about a mutual fund, an index fund, or an individual stock.

If, for example, you held Exxon stock and experienced a loss in its value, you can generate a capital loss by selling it. The IRS rules say that as long as you sell it and you're out of that position for thirty days, you can claim a loss. Then, if you wish, you can buy it back on day thirty-one.

If you don't like the idea of staying in cash that long, you can buy into another stock, or a mutual fund or an energy index fund perhaps in this case, or whatever you like.

Capital losses offset capital gains, so if you had other positions during that tax year that generated gains, your losses will help to offset them. Then, if there's anything left over, you can roll it forward indefinitely. Say you generated $50,000 in capital losses through these trades, and you also had $10,000 in gains during the year. A full $10,000 of that gain is now wiped out. You've still got $40,000 left over, and you can write $3,000 of that off your ordinary income on page 1 of your return. The remaining $37,000 rolls forward to next year, when you can do it again.

History tells us that eventually the market recovers, but this allows you to reduce some taxes in the meantime.

Roth Conversions

Charles came to see me initially after he'd already done his big Roth IRA conversion, and he was very pleased with himself for taking charge of it. When I questioned him, I learned he'd converted several hundred thousand dollars. When I started walking him through the mess he'd inadvertently made, his face fell. He'd already had to pay 32 percent of that pretax money in taxes, so that was a third of his money lost to tax. Now, he needed to consider how long it would take to get enough tax-free growth to get back into the green—a very long time, and he'd have to add in $700 a month in two years for his and his wife's Medicare premium surcharge to make it to breakeven—essentially another $9,000 in taxes. He'd made an expensive mistake and decided on the spot not to manage his own money going forward.

Decisions like this have all kinds of ramifications and unintended consequences, and like so many things in life, there are no do-overs. Please, don't rush into anything this impactful without reviewing what it will cost you and balancing that against what you gain.

Qualified Charitable Distributions and Donor-Advised Funds

As we get along in life and consider what kind of legacy we'd like to leave behind, many of us want to find ways to give back some of what we've been blessed with to charity. This, too, has an impact on your taxes—fortunately to your advantage in some situations.

Qualified charitable distribution (QCD) allows individuals aged seventy and a half or older to exclude from gross income up to $100,000 from their IRAs that is paid directly to a qualified charity. The excluded amount can be used to satisfy any RMDs. This was created because retirees can often no longer itemize given the large standard deduction.

Donor-advised funds (DAFs) can allow you to make contributions to charity and also receive a large up-front income tax deduction. This product allows you to make several years' worth of charitable gifts up front. This can be helpful in a year when you've got especially high income—for instance, if you get a retirement or severance package from your employer the year you retire. That can put you into a higher tax bracket. But if you open a DAF, you can put several years' worth of donations into that account and take a tax deduction of the entire amount in the year you're going to be more heavily taxed. You haven't actually given the money to charity yet; it's just in a holding account, and you can dole it out to your preferred qualified charity at whatever rate you like. You can deduct a maximum of only $10,000 in tax now, so if your standard deduction is $29,000, you would need to have a lot of mortgage interest and then contributions to get you over that hurdle.

This works really well for clients who are already regular givers to their favorite charities or church, because they were already planning to continue those donations and this offers them an advantage in a year when they'd otherwise have lost much more to taxes.

Some of the advantages include the following:

- Contributions to the fund are immediately tax deductible, subject to adjusted gross income limits.
- Contributions of long-term appreciated securities can help you avoid capital gains taxes.
- Contributions to the fund are professionally managed.
- It allows you to recommend investment strategies with the potential for tax-free growth and increased giving opportunity.
- It allows you to easily track your charitable deduction for that year.

- You can name counselors and successors to your account to continue the tradition of giving beyond your lifetime.
- You can determine whether you wish to receive recognition for your grants or remain anonymous.

Moving to Another State?

When we're getting ready to retire, we often focus on where we'd like to live—what part of the country is most appealing or where the weather is best. Mostly I see people considering the lifestyle changes, and it's exciting to compare one place with another and look at potential benefits to a big move—but when you're considering a move, you really want to include the tax changes in your calculations. Some states don't tax retirement income, for instance, including IRA distributions: Alaska, Florida, Nevada, South Dakota, Tennessee, Texas, Washington, and Wyoming. Some states have no state income tax at all, like Texas and Florida.

I've seen people decide against moving somewhere because it has a state income tax, but they haven't really researched it. The fact is that at the end of the day, as in Texas and Florida, you're going to have to pay taxes one way or the other. In Texas, we have higher-than-average real estate tax, and we have sales tax. If you move to another state that does have a state income tax, you might actually pay less, because maybe you don't pay state income tax on retirement income there and you don't have a sales tax or high real estate taxes. Some states, like California, have higher tax rates overall. But look at all the taxes in a particular state that will impact you, not just income tax, as you make your top-ten list of places to retire.

Some of our clients want to retire abroad. When you leave the United States and move abroad, the rules change significantly regarding your taxes, your various retirement accounts, and your medical costs. A good example is Canada, where some of our clients have chosen to relocate. Canada has its own tax system but also its own security laws regarding investments. Once they move there, the clients are no longer able to maintain their US investment accounts nor are they able to get advice from their financial planner in the United States, because an individual's security and investment regulations are based on where they're domiciled. It's extremely rare to find someone who can work in both Canada and the United States. The workaround for this situation is that you have to have someone with power of attorney based in the United States, where your financial advisor is working from. Alternatively, you've got to start working with someone in Canada.

Different countries have different tax treaties with the United States, so in some places you'll continue to just pay your US tax on your US investment income and retirement income. And then there are other places where, if you're paying income tax in that country, you get a credit here for what you've paid there. There are many potential tax scenarios, so I strongly suggest that you do your due diligence before packing up your household and heading for Costa Rica. The grass isn't always greener!

Required Minimum Distributions

This is one of those areas where it's essential to keep up with the ever-changing laws or to have a professional who takes care of that for you, because the age at which you have to start making withdrawals from your retirement accounts changes often. It used to be that you had to begin taking them at age seventy and a half; then it was seventy-two. It's just been moved up to age seventy-three, and in 2035 it will change to seventy-five.

All these years, you've been putting money into pretax retirement accounts and getting tax deductions, but at some point the IRS will want its tax money, and that's why there are required distributions. The required distributions are the IRS saying, "You've gotten the tax benefit long enough. We want some of that money." It's a percentage that increases each year based on its mortality table of taking it out over your lifetime. The required percentage you need to withdraw starts off at about 4 percent, meaning that if you had $1 million in your retirement account, you've got to take out $40,000, and then each year that percentage increases just a little bit, as does the balance in your remaining IRA that it applies to.

Should you do so? It's helpful to see this process as part of a puzzle. Some people can certainly afford to retire at age fifty-five or even younger. To figure out the best choices, we have to look at the best way to put it together. If somebody retires before fifty-nine and a half and most of their money is in those retirement accounts that we need to be able to access, there are other ways to do it. One of these is called SEPP, or substantially equal periodic payment.

SEPP allows you to withdraw funds from your IRA before age fifty-nine and a half without an IRS premature distribution penalty. However, the SEPP payment must continue unchanged for five years or to age fifty-nine and a half, whichever is longer. If changes to increase or decrease the payment are made, you could owe taxes and a 10 percent penalty on all the distributions. This is definitely one to discuss with your wealth management professional before committing to it.

Some people hit a rough patch or want to invest the money in another way, and they can begin to make withdrawals earlier at as young as fifty-nine and a half without a withdrawal penalty of 10 percent. There are other provisions, too, that allow you to skirt that penalty, such as illness. You will still have to pay taxes, however.

Get a Pro to Help You Put the Puzzle Together

Life goes more smoothly if you take the time to figure things out ahead of retirement and then continue to adjust and rebalance your finances as your needs change. We look at your taxes, your income, your budget, and ways to make sure you're not paying too much or getting too much back at the end of the year. That's when we make choices around where you should be taking money from and where it should go and when we see what your actual spending is. Doing these annual tune-ups is hugely beneficial in the first few years and can keep our clients from stepping on any lurking tax land mines.

Smart tax planning is essential to a secure retirement, so please don't go the DIY route or make any big decisions about moving money around until you've talked to a professional. You've worked hard to put it all together, and now isn't the time to take your eye off the ball.

CHAPTER 3

Investing in Retirement

> *"Can I grow my income in retirement, or is it too late?"*
>
> *"What are the best strategies for investment at this stage of my life?"*
>
> *"How should my risk tolerance change?"*
>
> *"How and when do I start using the money in my investment accounts?"*

When Alex came to see me for his regular financial checkup, he was not a happy camper. I hated to see it but resisted the impulse to say the obvious thing: "I warned you about this."

A year or so previously, we'd had a discussion regarding his savings and investments. Alex was a savvy guy who had kept about 70 percent of his retirement savings in the stock market for many years and through multiple cycles of growth and contraction. We'd met through one of my clients, who had sent Alex to me with questions about how to generate more income from his portfolio and how to manage his changing tax status. He had been an attentive listener, asked smart questions, and took notes. But on one big issue, he had already made up his mind. He was comfortable with his level of risk, one he'd held to for thirty or so years, and he wasn't interested in lowering it. He'd done well, was confident that he'd continue to do so, and was willing to weather the occasional market storm in pursuit of greater profits.

"Alex, the market doesn't care that you've retired," I cautioned. "The only certain prediction about the stock market is that it will go up and down. It's impossible to predict how much it will shift or exactly when, but market cycles happen, and your timeline for risk is changing with retirement—or it should be. Those downturns feel different when you no longer have a paycheck and are depending on your portfolio."

But no matter how many charts I showed him and how many scenarios I walked him through, Alex was resolute. He appreciated my efforts, but he'd come in with his mind made up, and nothing I could say would change his thinking. That was in 2021.

The Alex sitting across from me in 2022 had a very different view. The S&P 500 was down 22 percent, and NASDAQ had dropped 33 percent. The bond market, usually up in a down stock market, was down 13 percent—a kind of perfect storm. His portfolio had taken a beating, and the Alex I met with was a sadder but wiser man. In fact, he was rethinking his decision to retire—and that's a hard thing to face when you've happily left the working world behind.

Behavioral Finance and Plan B

As is true in so many aspects of our lives, what's worked in the past isn't guaranteed to work for us now or in the future. Alex had been comfortable with his level of risk as a working person, but he'd been brought up short by the impact of his new retired lifestyle on his ability to weather a hard downturn. The market had cratered before, certainly, but to Alex it hit differently now that he didn't have that paycheck coming in. We were able to course correct sufficiently to keep him from having to go back to work, but he wouldn't be spending as much as he had been for a while, and some of the plans he'd made had to be postponed.

What is "behavioral finance"? It describes the mindset in which you as an investor have been comfortable with market volatility in the past. While you were working, you had the luxury of simply not opening your statements during downturns. Why upset yourself? You knew that the right thing to do was to hang in there and wait for it to recover. When you're retired, you don't have that luxury anymore. You're living off your returns to some extent, and when they retract, it's ugly.

> Sure, what goes down will go up—but when? Because it's impossible to predict the market's timing with any accuracy, we need a solid plan B to provide for lost income.

As I said before, the market doesn't know you've retired, and these market declines are unavoidable when you're putting all your eggs in that basket. That's why I urge my clients to have a plan B, which means having enough money (apart from investments in the stock market) to cover living expenses for ten years while they wait for the market to recover. It may bounce back faster than that, but why hang your future security on a "maybe"?

Say you have a $1 million portfolio. If you have half of that in stocks, you've got the other $500,000 safely away from the market, money that you can live on while you wait for the market to recover. In a nutshell, that is plan B. The proportions and amounts may vary depending on what your income needs are and what kinds of other assets and retirement income you have. If your pensions and Social Security cover most of your expenses, you will probably need less. But knowing you're covered and that you don't need to start looking for a job or living on less (possibly much less) is a tremendous comfort.

Another client of mine had nearly all his money in one stock—the oil company for which he'd worked for many years and where he was a high-level exec. Altogether it was a hefty nest egg, and he felt assured of a safe and comfortable retirement.

Until the oil spill.

His company's stock sank like a stone and took his retirement with it. It would take years for the company to repair its reputation and make restitution for the damage the spill caused, but it would be okay eventually. For him, it upended and reshaped his retirement for the rest of his life. His portfolio lost a third of its value in a few days, and he would never get it back. Let this be a warning against having too much of your money not only in stock, but in any one stock.

"Is It Too Late for Me to Invest?"

Not at all! In fact, if we're going to protect and grow your nest egg rather than just draw it down or watch it get eaten up by inflation, you're going to need some investments. For most people who are retiring in their fifties or sixties, we look at their holdings as a thirty-year portfolio, because we want to see a growth component in their assets that helps them keep pace with inflation. I do meet with people who initially assume that it has to be all or nothing, but honestly that's not the best approach for most folks.

FUN FACT: THE RULE OF SEVENTY-TWO

No, this isn't the new Dan Brown novel. It's a mathematical formula that helps you understand how much growth you need to look for in your investments in retirement. Here's how it works. Start with your rate of return. Take that number and divide it into seventy-two. The number you get is how long it will take your portfolio to double. For instance, if you have a 10 percent rate of return, it will take about 7.2 years to double your portfolio.

And you can use the same factor to figure in inflation. If you have an inflation rate of 4 percent, you divide seventy-two by four and arrive at eighteen—so you know that every eighteen years, your cost of living is going to double.

Why does this matter? Because many people come to me with a misconception regarding their retirement savings. They assumed that the nest egg with which they retire is as big as it will ever get and that it's going to inevitably go down from there. But that won't work, because you can't continue to draw down if the market isn't cooperating, and inflation is going to wallop you over time, so you'll need to take more.

The bottom line is, it's not too late for you to invest, but your investment style might need an update if you've been either too conservative or too aggressive.

We've got software that lets us look at the allocation of individual portfolios through the lens of how they would have fared in any of the various historical market downturns. Looking at those results can really change your thinking. If you started with $1 million and lost a third of it in a few days, as has happened to others, it certainly gives you pause—or it ought to—and an incentive to rethink your attitude toward the market.

What Are the Best Strategies for Investment in Retirement?

With any thirty-year investment portfolio, including your retirement investments, investing is actually not that different from the way you'd previously invested. Figure out your asset allocation, get invested, stay invested, and periodically revisit and rebalance—the same core principles, but now with more attention to risk. I'd strongly suggest, though, that rather than doing it yourself, you entrust your portfolio to a wealth manager. I meet a lot of new clients who'd been managing their own portfolios over the years and who aren't necessarily keen on the idea of handing over the reins to someone else, and I get that.

But here's the thing: None of us is getting any younger, and it's possible that your mental acuity will suffer as you age, along with your energy and focus. Do you really want the responsibility of keeping that job on your plate? What if one spouse—the one who's been handling the finances—passes away? Who will help the surviving spouse understand and make decisions about your allocations? It's something to seriously consider, and so is the sense of relief you get when it's no longer your job but a professional's.

For most people, a mix of mutual funds, stocks, and bonds is appropriate, weighted correctly for your stage of life. We favor lower-cost investments; all wealth managers have the same products and tools at their disposal, but there are choices to be made, and that's where the difference is among us. Are we putting you where you need to be?

Don't get caught up in going after the shiny new thing that you've heard about that promises big payback with minimal risk, because that thing is a unicorn, and as we all know, unicorns are mythical beasts. If something seems too good to be true … but you know the rest. Likewise, if the investment as described is too complicated for you to understand, stay away from it. If your wealth manager isn't willing to make their choices and reasoning clear to you, stay away from them too.

Typically, my mix would look something like this: close to 80 or 85 percent of a portfolio in low-cost index funds, maybe 5 percent in other alternative products, and about 10 percent in mutual funds.

Actively Versus Passively Managed Index Funds—Which Is Better?

Actively managed index funds cost more to own because they require more attention. Say you want to invest in home improvement stores. Do you want to pay someone to decide whether you should own more Home Depot or more Lowe's? If you're good with owning an equal amount of both and leaving it there, you strip out the extra cost that comes with having someone make decisions about how much of each you need, as is the case with an actively managed fund. You may be willing to do so if you're looking for a greater return and you feel an active manager can offer that. But be aware that the increased costs may be offset by how much more you're paying the fund manager to do that for you.

That said, certain kinds of investments *do* need active management. One of the top-performing holdings I included in some portfolios last year was actively managed, because that year was a challenging one for the market. By having a brain behind the investment, my client was able to preserve capital and eke out a rate of return that beat the index, even though everything was mostly down.

Another kind of investment that probably requires an active manager's attention would be international bond funds if you want those in your portfolio. Why? Because someone needs to be aware of how any of those holdings might be impacted—by unrest, default, or some other kind of political/social/financial turmoil—in the specific countries. That fund manager needs to decide whether that country's bonds are a safe bet and, if not, get them out of the mix.

How I Build the Right Portfolios for Our Clients

Typically when I meet with a new client, the first step is a thorough assessment of what that person has in their portfolio. What ratio of stocks to bonds is in there? We discuss market volatility and how it has impacted them in the past. We talk about what their expectations are; if they have only 50 percent in stocks and the market is up 10 percent, they're probably not going to be up 10 percent, and it's important to be realistic. If they want a chance at higher returns, they need to be aware of the higher risk entailed. Depending on their answers, we craft an appropriate mix of holdings.

It's not as simple as a fifty-fifty split between stocks and bonds. Even with that mix, one portfolio could be a very aggressive one if the stocks held are small caps, internationals, real estate, and commodities or sectors. Another portfolio with the same kind of fifty-fifty split in which the stocks are mainly blue-chip large-cap company stocks is going to be more conservative.

For us, when it comes to retired clients, capital preservation is just as important as capital appreciation—and that's the biggest change for most folks in terms of retirement investment philosophy. When you're in the stage of accumulating assets, you're worried about appreciation. But once we shift into no longer having employment income and are dependent on that portfolio, capital preservation is just as important as appreciation.

"What Should I Do with My Required Distributions?"

When our clients have to take required distributions, if they're living off their portfolios, we build that into their monthly income and send what they need to cover the shortfall. But many of our clients either don't need the full amount they have to take or don't need it at all. In cases like that we may look at things like charitable strategies—the qualified charitable distribution. We'll have a conversation in the fall about how much we're required to take, what should be reinvested for them in a nonretirement plan account, and how much we need to withhold for taxes.

How do you start accessing the money in your portfolio? There are several strategies. The one we use most often is called *reverse dollar-cost averaging*.

Most folks who are adding to a retirement account are doing so by saving a certain portion of their paycheck each month, directly out of their paycheck to their 401(k). Some months they're buying when the market's low, sometimes when it's high—but regardless, they're putting away the same amount of money every month. Over time, that's what's called *dollar-cost averaging* because they're buying more or fewer shares depending on market price fluctuations. Reverse dollar-cost averaging is the opposite of that. I'm not deciding on a number and selling holdings from the portfolio to pay out over several months, because if I do that, I've lost time diversification because I'm banking all that on the January 1 price. If we need to take $24,000 from the portfolio by January 1, what we'd do instead is take $6,000 every quarter and then send you the $2,000 you need per month. That way we're selling a smaller amount from the portfolio at a time and spreading out those purchase prices.

These kinds of choices have a powerful impact on your financial health in retirement, which is why we think it matters whether you look at managing your portfolio as something you want to leave to an expert or tackle yourself. The DIY approach has appeal to some folks, but at this point in your life you're playing for keeps and can't count on the market bouncing back if you bet wrong.

Are you looking for a strategic investment plan that helps to build and protect your wealth? As part of our comprehensive approach to advice, we can help you formulate an investment strategy that can strengthen your portfolio and that suits your risk tolerance. We'll work with you to track and manage your investment strategy along with all the other things that are important to the full picture of your financial life. Sound investment strategy can help you have the confidence to enjoy the full and rich life you've earned today, tomorrow, and well into the future. We continually track the investment environment to help you appropriately position your portfolio, take advantage of current opportunities, and mitigate losses. When market conditions change, you can remain confident that the portfolio and plan we built together was designed to factor in market fluctuations.

"What About Annuities?"

I get asked a lot about annuities, and it's easy to see why. They're heavily advertised and, in some cases, promoted by financial advisors.

Promise people a regular return on their investment and a guaranteed income, and you'll get their attention. But there are many, many flavors of annuity, and not all of them are as great as they may initially look. I'm frankly not a fan, although I am a fan of monthly income. Annuities can be expensive and can limit your rate of return.

Sometimes people are offered a kind of annuity as an option for their pension when their employer offers them the choice of either a lump sum or a monthly payment. There's no one right or wrong answer that fits every case. Again, if we knew exactly how long we'd live, choices like this would make themselves, but I tend to prefer the monthly income because it's guaranteed. That frees us up to design your portfolio to do what it's supposed to do—continue to generate income. But in terms of taking a piece of your portfolio and using it to purchase an annuity, I'd advise going forward with extreme caution. All those bells and whistles come with a cost, and often the terms are difficult to understand. There are restrictions; you may lose the ability to cash out, usually for a long period of time, for instance. When people ask me about them, I tell them to ask a lot of questions and to not be embarrassed if they don't understand the answers. Make sure you're clear on what you're being offered and exactly what the conditions and restrictions are. Ask, too, about taxes on your annuity, because that can be a factor in your decision. And remember, if it sounds too good to be true … well, you know the rest.

We find that early on in retirement, people tend to spend a little more than they do in later years. Why? Maybe they're traveling more and for longer or have been waiting to buy a new car or to have work done on the house. If those folks can afford it, we're likely to send them a little more in these first months to cover those kinds of new expenses. On the other hand, if they're nervous about spending or tell us that they don't need that extra money, we'll reinvest it. But the point here is that you're not really going to know what your budget will be until you've experienced it, and that's something we help our clients recognize, adjust to, and learn to enjoy.

As I tell my clients, if you don't spend it, your kids will! While you're relatively young and healthy, do the things you've been dreaming of, because chances are that you won't want to when you're older and less energetic. Been longing for a kitchen remodel? Now's the time, because you're not going to care about that when you're eighty. Think a pool would look great in your backyard? Get it in before you're too old to want to swim in it. You've worked hard, saved smart, and earned your retirement goals. Go get 'em.

Investing will feel different to you when you're retired than it did when you were working. Understand your new risk tolerance. Don't be afraid to spend what you need to!

CHAPTER 4

Protecting Your Estate

> *"How can I prepare my loved ones for my passing?"*
>
> *"Do I have enough to leave my loved ones?"*
>
> *"How do I avoid spending my kids' inheritance or burdening them with it?"*

Alicia showed up at our offices without an appointment, something that rarely happens, as we typically book meetings several weeks out. When we got a call from the receptionist telling us she was here, we were surprised; we knew who she was, but we'd only ever met with her husband, Mike, so we didn't have any relationship with her. What could have brought her in today?

We went out to the lobby to greet her, and she told us that Mike had passed away unexpectedly. We were stunned—he'd been in just a few weeks before and had seemed in great health. Now Alicia was on her own and panicking. She had no idea where their money was or how much they had. All she had was our address, so she'd come on up looking for help. She was in awful shape, poor woman, just crushed with grief at her loss. Of course, we sat down with her and asked how we could help.

Mike had handled everything, she explained, in terms of finances. He'd paid all the bills, managed their money, and done all the banking. She honestly didn't know what bank he used, what accounts they had or where they were, or how much money she'd have to live on. They'd had a good life, a nice home—would she have to sell it now that he was gone? How would she live?

We were glad to be able to reassure her that she was going to be fine, financially at least. They were modest spenders and had a good net worth. The big challenge now was to bring her up to speed in terms of her financial literacy. She didn't know how to pay bills or even how to tell them from junk mail. She didn't know she'd have to pay real estate taxes. She didn't have a credit card in her own name—how would she get one? There was a lot she needed to learn, and we were happy to meet her where she was, because our job is to help our clients understand their finances, whatever their base level of knowledge is to start with. We sat down with her and came up with a plan to make the financial part of this transition as smooth as it could be.

Usually when we meet with clients, we talk about things like allocation, risk, and their portfolio statistics. Some of our clients don't want to get into the finer points or to have much, if any, involvement in how their money is managed; they just want to talk about their vacations and hear from us that they're in a good financial place. Alicia was worried that we'd expect her to become as financially astute as her late husband had been, but as with any of our clients, all we wanted was that she should get to a level of understanding that she was comfortable with.

Don't Leave Your Partner in the Dark!

We see situations like this more often than we'd like, because so often in a long relationship, one person shoulders the responsibility for managing the couple's finances and the other never learns the basics. This works fine until something happens to the person in charge of the money. Then their spouse is left in the dark, and the dark can be scary.

Mike had been a great husband who had made sure to set up a solid estate plan and put everything in order well ahead of his passing. The one thing he hadn't done was to share this information with his wife, and that wasn't good planning. I realize that some spouses aren't comfortable with that kind of discussion, but it really needs to happen. When your spouse is already grieving, why leave them with another awful unknown to cope with?

We often give our clients booklets that we call *Estate Planning Locators* to prevent this kind of confusion. In effect, they're do-it-yourself guides for the surviving partner or heirs that tell them what they need to know regarding the financial arrangement of the estate. They cover everything from listing out the brokerage and bank accounts to funeral plan preferences and where to find the will. We encourage our clients to fill them out and share them with their partner, but so many people just aren't comfortable having that discussion. It's not fun to contemplate your own demise—but it feels good when you've completed the booklet and know that in the event of your death, your partner's life won't be as rough as it would have been had you not taken the time to share this critical information.

Historically, a lot of the financial planning investment side has fallen to the husband's side of the ledger—but statistically the husband is usually the first to pass on. If you're the one who manages the money, teach your spouse to do it too. Let them know where the accounts are kept, where important paperwork is stored, who your attorney is—everything they'll need to manage without you. Write it all down, put it in a file, and show them where the file is stored.

Take them in to meet your wealth advisors so they're familiar with them. Be specific about what you want in terms of funeral arrangements, because grieving family members are easy prey for funeral home salespeople pushing expensive products. And put it in your own writing! Family members will be reassured by that, and you can ward off potential strife over what your wishes are.

We were able to reassure Alicia and set her up with a personal bookkeeper to teach her about bill paying, when to expect tax bills, and how to manage her daily financial transactions. We couldn't heal her grief, but we could help make sure the lights stayed on and her security was assured.

Secure Your Partner's Financial Safety

If you are sufficiently financially secure to retire, you're probably secure enough financially to pass away without worrying about your partner's welfare. But some things can change in the event of your death that might make that harder for them. Some pensions, for instance, don't continue at your passing, so if your lifestyle is largely funded via a pension, that might leave your partner less secure. While the need for life insurance generally disappears in retirement, in a situation like that you might want to consider maintaining your policy or getting one that will cover the loss of the pension.

Remember, expenses don't go down as much as you might think in the event of a partner's death. The house costs the same to finance and to run. It's better to leave them a little more than you think they'll need than to leave them to struggle with less.

Some people worry about their legacy to their kids. They don't want to spend everything; they want to leave a substantial inheritance to their heirs. A life insurance policy that covers both parents rather than just one is a way to do this. I helped a lady do this before her husband passed, because she was fretting about spending too much and leaving too little. The policy we set up would pay $1 million to her sons when she, too, passed, so she felt good knowing that no matter what happened with their other assets, her boys would be taken care of.

Inherited Wealth Can Be a Blessing—or a Burden

A client of mine came in to discuss his estate planning. He explained to me that he didn't want to burden his children with his wealth. That isn't something we hear often, but it made perfect sense to me.

If we think about our careers and what they have meant to us as we moved through life—our successes and failures, the relationships built, the sense of self-worth we've earned thanks to what we've accomplished, whether through our employment or the job we've done raising our kids—that's a big part of our self-definition. It gives us both pride and purpose. Now think about what a big financial gift can do to a young person's motivation and how missing that part of the struggle to find our meaning that's so much a part of most of our lives can destroy it. I've seen it happen, and it's not what their loving parents had envisioned.

When young people come into a windfall of inherited wealth, it changes their thinking. Initially, they feel as though they can't possibly spend it and that they're effectively set for life. They become careless in how they conduct their lives and profligate in their habits. They get restless and dissatisfied because they're missing something they can't buy and can't seem to identify—a sense of purpose and the motivation to drive them forward into maturity. Five years later, that big windfall has flown. Now they're facing life without that buffer of money to cushion the trip, and they've accomplished nothing, while their peers are establishing themselves and living like adults. And this isn't just younger adults but those who are older too.

"Easy come, easy go" is a truism for a reason. You or I wouldn't look at our retirement accounts in that way because we know very well how much effort went into building that wealth. Unless you win a lottery, you don't jump from zero to $1 million overnight. It takes years to build that kind of wealth. That knowledge keeps us from living frivolously and makes us more protective of our dollars.

But if you give someone something for nothing, they don't value it in the same way.

Recently we had a client in this position. When his widowed mother passed, this man in his mid-twenties was a primary school teacher and was self-supporting. He came to us to help him move the IRAs he'd been left into his own accounts and for advice on how to invest the funds.

It wasn't long before he called us, saying he wanted to buy a new car. His car was old and falling apart, and he felt strongly that his mother would have wanted him to get a new one. That required a withdrawal of $50,000 from the inherited IRA, because he'd have to pay around $15,000 in taxes. A few months later he decided that he wanted to spend his summer break in Europe, and there went another big piece of his inheritance. His taste for expensive trips and other things grew, as is usually the case when you get into the habit of lavish spending with money you didn't have to earn. It was just over three years before he'd run through it all—the whole nest egg his parents had worked so hard to grow and shelter.

How to Help Save Your Kids from Blowing Through Their Inheritance

Fortunately, there are legal financial instruments you can put into place to protect your children from making bad choices about spending what you've left them. One way is to leave money to your heirs in the form of a trust. Depending upon the state you live in, it may be a trust that you set up today, or in many cases it's just a trust that is a paragraph inside your will that states that instead of giving money to them outright, you give money to them in the form of a trust. Until they reach an age you specify, you appoint someone to be their trustee or co-trustee with them.

Trusts can be made as flexible or as inflexible as you want them to be. They can also help protect your heirs from losing that money in a divorce, bankruptcy, or judgment. Shared finances can get tricky when a marriage comes to an end, which is why it's important for your adult kids to keep that inheritance separate from shared money. Dividends get reinvested that were community property instead of separate property, and what belongs to whom gets muddied. The analogy I share with my clients is this: When you inherit dollars, picture that inheritance as a million-dollar bucket of white paint. But every time a dividend is reinvested to that portfolio—because that's income earned during the marriage—it's like putting a dollop of red paint into your bucket of white. Years into it, the marriage comes to an end and you and your spouse are in mediation over property. The judge looks at that bucket of formerly white paint and sees pink—because you've folded in those dividends and it's now impossible to separate what was the heir's property from their mutual property. So, the judge does what judges do and gives half of the pink paint to each partner. This isn't just the case with dividends. Perhaps you took some money out of the inheritance to buy a shared home in both your names or used community property funds to pay taxes on the investment accounts. You can see how quickly that can of paint turns pink, and that's why we keep that inheritance in a separate bucket and are very careful about its use.

Say disaster strikes; your adult child's spouse gets into a terrible car wreck that was his fault and goes into bankruptcy. The money within the trust is safe from lawsuits and liens and can continue to support them.

In most states it's easy to set up a trust, because it's really just a paragraph within your will. The hardest part is determining who will be the trustee, how long the trust will last, and the specific provisions you want to impose on the money and its distribution.

Should you use a revocable or an irrevocable trust? The situation I just described is typical of an irrevocable trust. Generally speaking, we are fans of revocable trusts if you live in or hold property in a state in which probate is a lengthy and often expensive process. But there are many states like Texas in which probate is inexpensive and quick, where you would end up spending more time and money than you need to with a revocable trust.

Where You Live Matters

It definitely matters when we're talking about what kind of trust you should have. And if and when you move to or purchase property in another state, you will probably need to update your estate plan to reflect the rules around trusts in your new home state and to make probate as seamless and inexpensive as you can.

The Statistics Around Inherited Wealth Are Sobering

You've spent years of your life putting together and preserving your wealth. It took hard work, thoughtful investments, and thrift to grow that nest egg, and you want to know that your heirs will respect that and be judicious in its use.

But don't count on it. The abstract of a 2013 study[1] done by Jay Zagorsky, currently a clinical associate professor in the Department of Markets, Public Policy, and Law at Boston University, revealed the following:

> Almost $4 trillion dollars of wealth is currently held by families with a life expectancy of less than 10 years. When that wealth is inherited, will it be retained or spent quickly? Results from the NLSY79, a longitudinal survey covering people in their 20s, 30s, and 40s suggest roughly half of all money inherited is saved and the other half spent or lost investing.

Most family assets are lost from one generation to the next because young people without life experience or financial expertise often splurge on expensive acquisitions—cars, boats, homes—without understanding what it costs to keep things up. And as I mentioned earlier, too much money too young can lead to young adults missing a big piece of the maturing experience that early struggles build.

You can help your adult kids do better. You may be uncomfortable sharing information with them about net worth or your estate plans, but it's a good way to help them become financially literate and

---

1 Jay Zagorsky, "Do People Save or Spend Their Inheritances? Understanding What Happens to Inherited Wealth," *Journal of Family and Economic Issues* 34, no. 1 (March 2013): 64–76.

learn to moderate their expectations and future behaviors. Letting them know about the details of the trusts, will, etc. is certainly a good way to go if you feel comfortable talking it over with them.

Prepare the Four Essential Documents

When you're putting together that file of essential information and documents for your surviving spouse and heirs, there are four documents you absolutely need to include there:

- Your will (make sure it's the most up-to-date version if it's been revised)
- Power of attorney
- Healthcare power of attorney
- Living will

You already understand why the copy of the will is important, but the others matter just as much.

Imagine that you've been sidelined by some catastrophic accident or illness and you're unable to make your wishes understood. You might be felled by a stroke or in a coma. The power of attorney you make out in advance of need can help your spouse or other trusted appointee in that they will be able to make financial decisions on your behalf and sign legal documents.

A healthcare power of attorney allows your spouse or someone else you appoint to make medical decisions on your behalf if you're unable to do so.

A living will stipulates your wishes in the case that you become incapacitated. You can stipulate the degree to which you want or don't want medical interventions. Do you want to be kept alive by artificial means, even if there's little or no chance of your regaining consciousness? Many of us find the idea repellant, but a loving spouse may not have the strength to tell the doctor to "pull the plug." Letting them know that is what you'd want takes that burden off their shoulders.

Many people find the idea of their own death or incapacity so frightening that they put off filling out these essential documents. But in doing so, they're doing their spouse and heirs a terrible disservice.

To whom should you give power of attorney? Often if you've got adult children, it goes to the youngest of them or, alternatively, to the one who lives closest to you. Again, this is something that should be discussed with your kids before it's needed. One may be happy to take that on, while another wants nothing to do with it. A client of ours had specified that his youngest daughter take it on; his reasoning was that she'd be the most likely to be healthy enough to manage it by the time he or his wife passed or were incapacitated. But that wound up causing strife with their older child, who lived in the same town with his parents and who had taken up the work of paying the parents' taxes, insurance, and other bills when they were no longer able to do so. He felt that handing power of attorney to his sister somehow suggested that his parents had found him less than trustworthy, and it caused real strife in the family.

Remember, the people who love you are going to be agitated and grieving when you become incapacitated or pass and won't be at their best. That's a hard time already, so do what you can ahead of it by making sure everyone knows where everything is ahead of time, who's in charge of what, and why you made those choices. And again, as with your will, revisit your essential documents when family members or you move, and adjust them accordingly. Good communication can prevent hurt feelings and family schisms, which certainly aren't part of the legacy you wish to leave behind.

Do Periodic Reviews of Your Accounts and Their Beneficiaries

It's critical to review how your accounts are owned as well as the beneficiaries listed on those accounts. I talked above about setting up trusts, but trusts need to be funded. If all our accounts have beneficiaries on them, those trusts are never funded because the beneficiaries supersede what the will says. You could have this beautiful trust written inside your will, but unless there are assets that are funneled through the will, meaning "the beneficiary is my estate," or there is no beneficiary, the trust is never funded.

If you want to avoid probate, that may be possible via what's called a living trust, depending on where you live. This can help in a situation where one of the spouses passes first and the other remarries. You may want to make sure that your kids and not that new spouse get the money you've left, and a living trust can be set up so that your widowed spouse gets the use of the money while they are alive, but on their death, it passes to your children, not the new husband or wife. If those accounts are held jointly by you and your spouse, they go to the surviving spouse and not through the trust.

Again, make sure to look at these arrangements every few years, because things do change. Discuss them and any changes you're contemplating with your financial advisor and estate planning attorney. Make sure things like bank names where the accounts are held are up to date.

It's a good idea to keep individual checking accounts for each spouse funded with enough cash to get your spouse or yourself through those first few weeks until things settle down. Banks may freeze the assets in a joint account, and you don't want to be unable to pay your bills in the meanwhile.

If you or your spouse do not have your own credit cards, get one for each of you apart from whatever cards have both your names on them. Why? Because credit cards are never really jointly owned. You may have put your spouse on the card as a secondary user, but the actual account is in one person's name, and if your primary account holder passes and the bank finds out, it will freeze that card. We've met a lot of older adults who've never had a credit card or loan in their own names—and thus have no credit rating and are unable to get a card in their own names. This can be a massive inconvenience, especially in already stressful times, and is easy to avoid with some forethought. The spouse doesn't need to use that card often but regularly enough that a history of use and timely payments is built in their names.

We can't plan for everything that comes at us, but when we're talking about protecting our estates, simple steps like the ones described in this chapter can go a long way to smoothing out troubling times for your family when you're gone. Don't put off the process of estate planning, because life is an uncertain proposition, and the people you love deserve better. Let them know about the decisions you've made, and be sure to consult with them before you appoint them to any position of responsibility like executor or power of attorney.

CHAPTER 5

Summing Up: When Is the Right Time to Retire?

> *"What dates do I need to know about before I retire?"*
>
> *"What dates do I need to know about after I retire?"*
>
> *"How do laws impact me at different ages?"*

I've given you a lot of food for thought in the previous chapters in the interests of getting you to a fuller, more comprehensive understanding of the financial, legal, and tax ramifications of retirement. Let's look at some of the key topics we've discussed and consider your all-around retirement readiness.

Things to Consider When You're Weighing Retirement

- *Can you afford to retire?* We've covered this ground pretty extensively, so you should have a solid base on which to assess your financial retirement readiness. This isn't the time to go with a DIY approach, though, so you need to check your numbers and calculations with a wealth management professional before making the leap to retirement. You may want or need to work part time or independently for some time rather than go cold turkey. Remember, it doesn't have to be "all or nothing."

- *What are your family obligations?* Do you still have children to raise or to put through school? Are you supporting or financially assisting other members of your extended family? How will these obligations change in the coming years?
- *How invested are you in your career?* Is it still exciting and something you want to stick with, or are you done? Are there other areas you'd like to explore as stopgaps, like consulting or other kinds of work in retirement, or are you ready to just "do you"?
- *How's your health?* No matter how well we are, life is a limited proposition, and statistics tell us that sooner or later we'll be faced with health challenges that may be debilitating or worse. Knowing that you're closer to the end of your life than you are to the beginning, use that knowledge to put your personal priorities first. What do you want to do with this precious time? How and with whom do you want to spend it?

"Ready" Looks Different to Everyone

You're the only one who can define what your retirement looks like—and it's important to realize that at different points in your life, what it looks like will change. For some people, retirement is barely a blip in their activities. It's less of a rest or extended vacation than it is a chance to reinvent themselves via the active pursuit of a beloved hobby, a new career, or full-throttle volunteer work, and those folks will probably be as busy (if not busier) than they were when they were working. For others, it's an opportunity to hit the pause button as they consider the spectrum of options in front of them.

Remember that adjustment to retirement is part of the process—a feature, not a bug—and in my observation, settling into your new life requires a *minimum* of a year. For many of us, it takes more time than that, and a few of us never really get comfortable with it. But as with all things in life, it's a question of attitude, and when you retire, give yourself the grace to flounder a little bit before you feel comfortable with the new normal.

If you find yourself struggling or depressed, there's no shame in it. Do what you'd reasonably do when faced with any kind of health issue: Seek out help from a professional. Talk therapy can be a great way to air your fears and examine them with the help of a dispassionate professional.

Many people use their "bad" days as a reason to hit the gym. Exercise releases feel-good hormones in the brain, keeps you limber and fit, and provides some social interaction. Consider investing in a personal trainer for added accountability and engagement.

It's important to keep your sense of agency and effectiveness. You're in the driver's seat now, so don't be afraid to take the wheel. You can always course correct down the road.

Critical Dates and Age Markers

There are some important ages and dates to keep in mind when it comes to managing your retirement income and investments. Since this is an area in which you might easily step on a tax land mine, these need to be on your radar and your calendar.

KEY DEADLINES YOU NEED TO KNOW

AGE 50 You can make "catch-up" contributions to retirement plans (if the plan allows).

AGE 55 This is the age at which you can withdraw from your 401(k)s if you wish to do so, without penalty, if you left that employer in the year you turned fifty-five or later.

AGE 59½ Penalty-free withdrawals from IRAs and qualified retirement plans are allowed at this age.

AGE 62 You may choose to start receiving Social Security or to put it off, depending on your situation. Discuss your best choices on this with your wealth management advisor and tax professional before you decide. At this age, your payment will be discounted to account for the additional years of payments.

AGE 65 You become eligible to apply for Medicare.

AGE 66-67 You can apply for Social Security and get your full benefit, depending on your birth year. Remember, delaying your payment to age seventy will maximize your monthly payment given that you will receive fewer years of payments.

AGE 70½ (QCD age)—At this age, individuals aged seventy and a half or older are allowed to exclude from gross income up to $100,000 from their IRAs that is paid directly to a qualified charity. The excluded amount can be used to satisfy any RMDs.

AGE 73 (Rising to seventy-five in 2033)—This is the age at which you must start taking your RMDs if you have not already done so.

"But What If I Need Money Earlier Than the Deadlines Listed Here?"

If you're retiring early—before age fifty-nine and a half—there are ways to access your IRAs, retirement plans, and nonqualified annuities without incurring that punitive IRS penalty tax. Of course, this is only done in cases of real need, and you want to avoid using that money if possible. But when you must, you must, and the means is called SEPP. This stands for substantially equal periodic payments, which I discussed in chapter 2.

Using SEPP, participants in IRAs and employer-sponsored retirement plans and owners of nonqualified annuities can avoid the IRS 10 percent premature distribution penalty tax by taking out specific payments over a period of time. Once SEPP begins, the payout method chosen must continue without modification (other than by reason of death or disability) for five years from the date of the first payment or until age fifty-nine and a half, whichever is longer. (Qualified plans have a ten-year restriction.) If payments are modified or stopped prematurely, the taxpayer is liable for a 10 percent penalty (plus interest) on all prior distributions and for the interest on the tax obligation avoided during the years that distributions were made. SEPP is defined in section 72(t) of the Internal Revenue Code.

In all cases, please consult with your tax professional and wealth management specialist before making any choices or changes. As I've noted before, tax laws change almost annually, and a mistake can be costly.

Other Dates to Consider as You Plan

Is there a big project on your desk at work that needs completing? If so, decide whether you want to wrap it up before you retire or prefer to bring a colleague or new hire up to speed so they can take it over.

If a big project is coming up or a major company reorganization is about to begin, consider timing your retirement so that you can be out of there and your replacement can hit the ground running.

Once we've gone over the numbers and established that, yes, you are financially secure enough to retire and you're ready to do so, most of us start the process by a gradual but definite pulling away from our jobs in multiple ways. First, we make practical adjustments, whether on our own volition or because our employers request or require us to do so. We pass on institutional knowledge to the person who'll be taking on our duties or to HR. We give our ongoing projects over to others to see to completion and help them understand the complexities and issues they'll need to address in order to do so. We look at our list of responsibilities and make sure that whoever is stepping into our shoes has that list too—or that HR does if a new hire isn't yet in place. We pack up our personal items and take them home. We go through our files and forward those that the next person in our job or others there might need. We shed the skin of this old existence, and it's liberating.

Emotionally we're pulling away too. Unless we're the business's founders, we're likely to be thinking less about the company we're leaving and more about the life we're moving toward. We're happy to see those responsibilities go to someone else, because they seem more burdensome now than they have in the past. It's harder to concentrate on the job in these few days remaining, and we may find ourselves daydreaming, impatient to be out of there and on to the next adventure.

Intellectually our focus is on the change we're about to step into, so the to-do lists and calendar entries we're making have more to do with the future than the present or past. That last week or two gives us the chance to decompress, to review, and to open up to the untrammeled beauty of new horizons and a freer life.

Is there a "best time" to retire from your particular company insofar as considerations like accrued vacation days, vesting for stock options, or pension calculations are concerned? Talk to your peers and to HR. You don't want to leave money on the table!

Bottom Line

Keeping up with the changing tax laws and regulations around retirement income is a full-time job in itself, and I strongly advise to you seek out qualified professional help before you make any decisions, including your retirement date. There are a lot of moving pieces in these calculations, and you don't want to make a costly error. Find an experienced CPA and financial advisor to work with you and help you plan your exit strategically.

In the next section of the book, we'll talk about how to make sure this fresh start is the best and brightest we can make it.

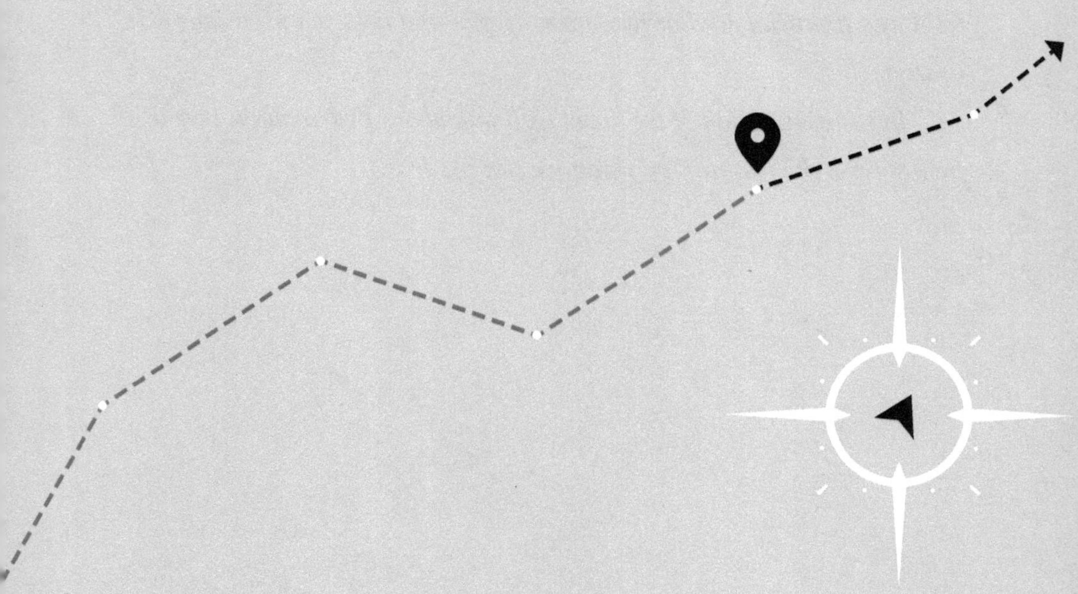

PART II
Retirement in Color

You've built a great retirement portfolio; you've saved, invested, and planned for this new chapter, and you're set to enjoy life on your own terms. Good work! You've certainly earned this, and financially you're as ready as you can possibly be.

But there's more to a successful retirement than having your financial security assured—a lot more. And if you're not thinking into the lifestyle shift you're about to experience, you risk becoming one of those unfortunate folks who *fail* retirement.

Yep, I said *fail*—because if you've put all this attention into guaranteeing your fiscal health but little or no thought into how you're going to live this new life and embrace the change, real contentment may elude you. This part of your life—the "soft skills" part—requires planning and investment just as your financial security did.

I'm going to address these skills and how to refresh or develop them in this second half of the book, but don't assume that because it's the second half it's any less critical to your future than the first half. I've seen people fail retirement, and it's not pretty. The guy who kept going back to work, not for the money but because he felt so purposeless without a job. The couple whose dreams for this part of their lives turned out to be so divergent that they split up after a forty-year marriage. The couple who sold their longtime home and relocated to a new state for the lifestyle—and then discovered how hard it was for them to make new friends and wound up moving back to their former town (and taking a loss on their home sale). These were very different people, but they'd all made the same mistake. They'd neglected to game out their postretirement lives, and consequently they failed at retirement.

Yes, life does change after retirement—and you've got to be prepared to change along with it. Routines, schedules, activities—everything's different, but you're still the same. Expect some friction and a few bumps as you make the adjustments to your new life. Growth is sometimes painful, but you can't avoid it.

Embrace it. Get out ahead of the challenges by thinking through what you want out of this next chapter, discussing it all with your partner, and identifying the possibilities before you commit to anything big.

I can't give you all the answers, but in this section I'll help you define and explore the questions that will take you there.

CHAPTER 6

"Location, Location, Location ... Where Should I Live?"

> *"Where will I be happy?"*
>
> *"Can I afford to live where I want to?"*
>
> *"What should I consider when deciding where to live?"*

One of the topics our clients bring up the most often when we talk about their retirement plans is where they want to live now that they're free to move. For many, moving has been a longtime dream, and they're eager to pull up stakes and make that dream their new reality.

There are many reasons to consider a move—but the assumptions made about how a particular move will improve someone's life aren't always completely sound once we dig into them.

"I Love It There in Summer!"

Many of our clients flee the Houston area in the summer when the heat and humidity reduce much of daily life to dashes between air-conditioned spaces. Carol was one of them, and for her, it was Maine, specifically the Bar Harbor area, where her idea of paradise was to be found. Summer and early fall were delightful, and she'd always left the area regretting that she had to return to sweaty Texas. Someday, she told herself, she'd buy a little house on the Atlantic coast and leave Houston behind for good.

"Have you ever been to Maine in January?" I asked.

She had not, but she told me that she liked the idea of snowy winters and the off-season quiet. My feeling was that aging bodies and navigating through months of ice and snow aren't an ideal match, but she was in the thrall of a dream, and we don't want to dismiss people's feelings. She was already weeding her belongings, she said, to get her place ready to show.

Instead of trying to talk her out of it altogether, I offered another idea. Why not talk to the person from whom she regularly rented or just find a place in the town she liked on one of the vacation home rental sites and see if she couldn't negotiate long-term rental? If you're interested in being in a vacation home during the offseason, you can often get significantly reduced rates and (assuming the home is winterized) get the experience of wintering in a summer town without uprooting yourself. It could save her a lot of hassle and potentially a lot of expense and heartbreak if the reality didn't live up to her expectations. She thought about this a moment and then nodded—she'd do as I advised and give it a try.

Good thing she did too. Having worked out an affordable deal with her Maine rental agent, she breezed through the summer and delighted in the nippy fall weather—but when winter hit, she realized how dark and isolating a time it was in a place where you had no close friends and just a handful of acquaintances. The restaurants she'd enjoyed in the summer mostly closed up for the season, and people hunkered down with their families. And getting around was a nightmare, she said, because she'd never really had to drive in northern winter weather, and it was a whole new ball game. She wound up cutting her lease short and coming back to Houston, thankful that her home was there waiting for her.

She briefly considered buying a vacation property up north but ultimately decided that she was happy with the seasonal rental arrangement she had and that if the Maine coast lost its fascination in a few years or she was no longer able to travel there easily, she was better off not having to sell a home she wasn't using.

If you're considering a permanent move to a place you've loved to vacation, think about doing what Carol did and "try before you buy." The place that's so busy and charming in the high season may turn into a ghost town in the offseason.

Now, if that summer or winter place is where you grew up, or if you have significant family or friends there, that can be a mitigating factor in your decision-making. Even so, seasonal renting might be your best option, and give it a good try before you go ahead and buy. *You Can't Go Home Again* is more than the title of a book by Thomas Wolfe; the fact is, the place where you grew up isn't going to be the same as it was when you lived there, and it may no longer hold the appeal it holds in your memory. Renting gives you the freedom to try out different options and different lifestyles without gambling your future happiness on a memory.

We worked with a couple who loved Chicago. They were both from there originally, and though they had lived many years in

Houston, they'd always wanted to go back. When they retired, they decided to make the move. They bought a beautiful condo and put a lot of effort and money into redoing it, which was fun for both of them and kept them occupied. But even for them, the winter was just too much. They missed their friends in Houston and the church they'd belonged to, and they missed golfing in February—so they wound up selling the condo and moving back!

Why? Chicago wasn't the same place it had been back when they'd lived there twenty-five years ago. They missed their friends, and walking the dog now required an outing rather than just sending him out into the backyard to play. This part of the retirement adventure ended up costing them dearly in terms of relocation costs, but fortunately their move back home made them happy. They'd have been happier still if they had simply rented and tried it out before taking the plunge.

Moving Means More Than Just a Change of Address

When we retire, a lot about our lives doesn't alter. Our circle of friends doesn't change, and our interests are likely to stay the same. If we love to craft or trail ride or play golf, we probably already have people we enjoy doing those things with and places we go to do them. When we move, all these things change in terms of who and where. That can be great, because change can be invigorating. But it's also challenging.

Consider the holidays. Will you be able to be with your family (if that's important to you and them) in this new place? Will it be easy for them to come to you if you're the ones who typically host the family gatherings? If your contemplated new home is in an exotic or faraway location, it may be expensive or otherwise impractical for your kids and their kids to travel to your home. Can your extended family afford to fly? Can they afford to take the time off to come? It can get difficult when they're working parents with kids in school. That's something you need to discuss well ahead of making any written-in-stone decisions, both with your spouse and your adult kids.

Then there are the practical considerations. Who will be your doctor? Where will you get your hair cut? Retiring to the Bahamas and spending every day in the sunshine sounds like a good idea, but it might not offer all the benefits you're truly looking for. You should sit down and discuss things like the following:

- *What is there to do in this new location?* Is it a seasonal place where most of the people pack up and leave in the offseason?
- *What's the year-round climate like?* Not just the high season but the rest of the seasons?
- *What medical facilities are nearby?* Having a good hospital close to you gets increasingly important as you age. You don't want to have to wait half an hour for an ambulance, much less travel an hour in one to the nearest full-service hospital. We've seen some of our Houstonites fulfill a dream of moving to the Hill Country but discover that the medical facilities there just don't compare to the world-class facilities offered in Houston.
- *How easy is it to see family and loved ones?* Will travel to visit each other be prohibitively expensive or too lengthy to be practical for families with young children?
- *How will you make friends?* (I'll talk more about this in a subsequent chapter.) If you have lived in one community for many years, chances are you've got a fairly robust circle of friends via your working colleagues, the families you met when your

kids were in school or playing sports, or other shared activities and interests.

Even Lee Iacocca admitted to having found retirement a tough transition, made more difficult by the decision to move. He said, "For me, pulling up roots was the hardest part. Moving from Michigan to California would have been difficult under any circumstances. Coming right at the moment when I used to run a company and then had to find something to do with my life, it was a double whammy."[2]

Anticipate Your Costs to Move

The costs involved in selling your current home and in moving your stuff to a new location are significant but are not the only financial considerations involved in a move. If you're moving from one community to another, perhaps to a new state or even a different country, your tax situation and cost of living are almost certainly going to change. It's important to assess what the differences will be and whether they're to your advantage.

How does this new location tax your retirement or other income? What are the rates of sales tax, real estate tax, or estate taxes? What about state income tax? Now, every state is going to have some form of taxation to support its services, but this can vary a lot, and you'll want to crunch the numbers and compare them with your current tax situation.

How do housing costs compare? How about the costs of groceries or meals out? If you need help maintaining your home, such as housekeeping or yard or pool service, how do the costs and availability of these services stack up to what you currently pay? Will they be within your means if you need them going forward?

---

2 Alex Taylor III and Lee Iacocca, "How I Flunked Retirement," *Fortune*, June 24, 1996.

Many people talk about downsizing, but in all honesty I have to tell you that for the most part, people actually make lateral moves in terms of costs and size of house. If you're looking at getting a smaller home, will that limit your ability to house visiting family or guests?

If you're used to living in a multistory home, consider switching to a single-story dwelling. In fact, as you look at homes, look at what they offer you in terms of aging in place. You don't want to have to move again if down the line you can no longer navigate steps. Similarly, you need to look at things like doorway widths, hall widths, and anything else that might make it difficult or impossible to get around your home if you're in a walker or wheelchair.

I can't stress too much the importance of trying out a new neighborhood before you buy into it. Nothing apart from actually living there for a longer term (in a rental!) will give you sufficient experience of the neighborhood, the shopping, the climate, the traffic—everything that contributes to or detracts from the quality of everyday life.

Will you need a different kind of car in this new place? A ragtop sports car isn't going to cut it in a New England winter. Factor in the cost of replacing your car. Maybe where you live currently you don't need a car and rely on walking or public transportation. Alternatively, maybe you're moving to a city but still want to have your wheels for day trips out of town. Parking is a big headache in most metropolitan areas and expensive to boot.

Some people look at the numbers and decide to buy a vacation home in their dream area rather than go full move. This can be a good alternative, but again, the costs may be prohibitive. Remember, a second home means you now have two sets of bills to pay along with the cost of keeping that home in good repair. Also, you may feel that because of the expenses you've assumed, you have to go there rather than do something else or visit a new place. That can be awfully limiting. Renting may be a better choice because you're not chained to a place you might no longer wish to or be able to enjoy.

"Should I Move Closer to My Kids?"

This is a question we hear often, and while I understand the appeal of such a move, there are some things you might want to consider before you commit.

First, how close is too close? For most people, living next door can turn out to be a mixed blessing, as you're likely to be pressed into service as babysitters. That might sound great, but do you really want to be the family's go-to? Half an hour away might make more sense, in that it gives both families their space but means you can see them more often.

Another issue is your adult child's career and life choices. They may not be married to the place they currently live. If they have a change of jobs that necessitates moving their family to a new community far from you, you're either going to be stuck or packing up yet again. Not ideal.

Sometimes living closer to your adult child and their family can create tensions and even friction between you all. A client of ours complained to me about how her son and his wife spoiled their children by buying them everything they asked for and how she and her daughter-in-law had had words about it. This wasn't what she and her husband had hoped for, certainly, when they decided to move, but it happens, particularly when a grandparent sees what they view as poor parenting choices being made. Here's the thing—you've already raised your kids. Now you've got to be able to stand back and let them raise their own children. Advice, however well intended, is not always welcome, particularly from in-laws. And your kids probably don't want you raising theirs.

One of the best tips I've heard on this topic is to put out the welcome mat and button your lip. Your job is to enjoy your grandchildren, and if your kids want advice, they'll ask for it.

Considering Adult Communities and Full-Service Senior Housing Facilities?

Adult communities are hugely popular, especially in places where the climate is friendly to year-round outdoor activities like golfing. We have several in the Houston area. They have definite advantages, particularly if you're getting to the age at which you no longer want the responsibilities that come with regular home ownership. Most of these are aimed at people fifty-five and up, and many find them a good choice.

Be sure to do some digging before you make the leap, though, as these communities tend to have fairly rigid rules for residents regarding things like having children as houseguests. One I know of limits child visitors to a couple of nights a month, which isn't enough for some folks. Talk to some people in the neighborhood and find out what their views about the place are. And again, don't neglect to check out the available medical care and other necessities before you make a choice. Some people love the homogeneity of a community like this, while others find it dull.

At a certain point in your life, you're likely to be ready to dispense with chores like mowing the lawn or keeping house. For people who want the guarantee that they can age in place for the rest of their lives, there are places called life plan communities. You generally have to buy into these places plus pay a monthly fee. Usually some, if not all, of your meals are included and served in common dining areas. You may have a condo, a cottage, or an apartment, and the degree of creature comforts offered varies depending on the community. Housekeeping is usually included, as are outings and access to some kind of local transportation to get around town if you need something. They may offer extensive programs for your enjoyment—trips out, exercise and craft classes, book clubs, even musical performances and guest speakers.

These facilities usually include nursing care and often dementia care for people as they age, which means that if you need a skilled nursing facility but your partner does not, they can stay in the apartment and you can move to another part of the campus. For many people, this kind of arrangement is a tremendous comfort, because they know that no matter what, they and their spouse will be cared for, and they won't be a burden to their children.

But they aren't for everyone. First of all, the nice ones tend to be expensive, though the cost can vary a lot depending on where in the country you live. The food and communal dining may not be to your tastes, but you'll likely fall back on it anyway since you're paying for it. There can be a tendency to shut out the outside world, since every effort is made to see to it that you don't need anything. And you may find that people don't visit you there as much as you'd like.

Bottom Line

Take your time, and don't rush into making a big change with a move in retirement. Explore your options carefully and with a critical eye. The grass is famously not always greener, even though it can look that way from a distance. Think about health and lifestyle factors before you make the jump, and sit down with your advisor and crunch the numbers. Moving can be a big adventure or a big headache. Do your due diligence, and look before you leap.

CHAPTER 7

Family Relationships in Retirement

> *"How do we keep love alive after a big change?"*
>
> *"How can my partner/spouse and I make time for ourselves and each other?"*
>
> *"What if we split up in retirement?"*

How will retirement impact your marriage/partnership? What about your relationships with your kids and grandkids? That's a seemingly simple question with multiple possible answers, not all of which are so uncomplicated.

Unless the two of you worked together, you and your spouse spent the better part of your working lives apart from one another. Sure, there were evenings, weekends, and vacations together, but your workweek occupied most of your waking hours and attention. It's likely that you've made meaningful friendships with your colleagues—and that your partner has with theirs—or with a circle of friends. Your respective workdays have been the topic of your dinner table talks, and the daily rhythms of working life have become as comfortable as old slippers.

Now, you're retired—and everything is different. One lady told me that the phrase she'd most dreaded came out of her husband's mouth his very first day home: "What's for lunch?" That's funny, but it wasn't amusing to her at the time. Like him, his wife had her own regular daily life, busy and productive and very much hers. How would they manage now, the two of them, cut loose from their routines?

As it turned out, they managed very well, because both of them were smart enough and committed enough to realize this was a new kind of normal that would take adjusting to. In some ways, it's like those first days of marriage, in that you're both trying to create a healthy blend of your two lives into a shared existence. As was the case at the beginning of your relationship, many things had to be negotiated. Who was responsible for what? Who took the lead in what areas, and was that the best choice? Were decisions made mutually, or did one person tend to dominate the conversation? Marriage is, after all, a contract, and one that is renegotiated many times over the course of a lifetime together. The continued health of the marriage depends on the fairness of that contract in all its iterations, because the best deal is one in which each partner feels they've been fairly treated. Many kinds of events can bring us to one of these marital turning points; the birth of a child, a big move, or a serious illness are just a few of the possible life events that can impact a relationship and require us to grow together to stay together.

Attitude Determines Altitude

As is true in so much of life, the attitude you bring to retirement will decide how well you weather it. If you're a naturally optimistic and flexible person, rolling with change comes easier for you than it would be for someone who's less sunny in their outlook and who doesn't handle deviations in routine easily.

If you're the optimist in a relationship, you're going to have to do some cheerleading and dig deeply into your store of patience and forbearance if your partner is your opposite in this regard. If you're the less flexible partner (and you know who you are!), be conscious of that and do your best to stay even keeled. If you find yourself getting flustered, impatient with your spouse, or feeling depressed and at odds with the world, look for ways to make it better. Talking with a therapist can help, as can regular exercise, which releases endorphins.

If you've had a career in management and are used to being the decision maker at work, remember that at home you're an equal partner, not the boss anymore, and act appropriately. Delegating the work of the home—who does what and how often—has to be a shared decision and isn't something one person can simply decide on and impose on their mate. If your mate has been the one who stayed home and kept your lives in order, they have their own schedule around the running of the house and how things are best done. Listen to them and be willing to accommodate yourself to their needs and preferences. Your retirement is a big adjustment for them too. You're coming into their world, and you need to respect their feelings.

It helps to look at this as a new beginning—like your early days together when you first married—because you're going through a similar process of mutual discovery and exploration. The great part is that you know and love this person already, and both of you have a much clearer view of each other's strengths and needs than you did at the start. Being thoughtful, listening to your partner, and remembering that they, too, have a routine that's going to change now is the best way to keep things going as smoothly as they can. Instead of asking what's for lunch, maybe offer to take them to lunch—or to make something for the two of you.

Why Do Some of Us Struggle with Retirement?

Most retirees are delighted with their new freedom and the opportunity to choose their own adventures. Unfortunately, not everyone makes the transition so easily. For some, "retirement" is synonymous with being relegated to the sofa or put out to pasture. They lose their sense of agency and their feeling that they have a purpose in the world. Sometimes, they sink into depression and withdraw into themselves.

It's not hard to understand how that can occur. Many of us didn't have great role models for retirement growing up. People didn't live as long we do today or with the degree of fitness and health we see in older folks now, so retirement was an end rather than a beginning. I've heard this phase of life compared to a midlife crisis, but in a way it's more challenging than that, because you're likely more than halfway through your life, so the choices you make seem that much weightier.

When a couple hasn't emotionally prepared for retirement, the marriage can suffer. Suddenly faced with much more "together" time, couples sometimes discover that in the intervening years, they've grown apart and are no longer interested in the same things. They're different people now than they were when they first fell in love; the kids have grown up and moved on with their lives, and the common concerns they'd shared with one another just aren't there anymore.

It's sad, but it happens. The best thing I can say about this is that in my observations, the few postretirement splits I've seen have been of the amiable variety, not the acrimonious kind. Settlements are worked out, and the couple go their separate ways. They don't necessarily dislike each other; they just want to do different things at this point in life. The love can still be there, but it's trumped by the mutual desire to try on other kinds of life choices, and that's okay.

Before making any kind of big, life-altering decision, please consider it carefully through the lens of the changes you're already experiencing and that may be impacting your ability to make good choices. There's no shame in seeking help or advice from a professional therapist (which I am *not*) when you're feeling at odds with yourself and the world.

Keep Communication Open and Flowing

There's no substitute for ongoing communication in a marriage, and that's never truer than when you're about to experience a big transition together. Instead of waiting until you've had your last day on the job, use the time you two have together before retirement to talk in depth about what each of you wants this new chapter of your lives to look like. Maybe one of you has anticipated that the other will join in with their hobbies now that there's time for that, but the other isn't interested and has plans of their own. Maybe you both want to take on a challenge—a home remodel, a big trip, a new hobby—together. Maybe one of you has a dream of taking a month in a little Italian village and taking language courses, or attending a cooking school in France, or making wine. Now's the time to air those long-deferred dreams and look for ways to share them. There's a whole world out there and time to explore it. Does your spouse know you plan on going fishing every day the weather allows and that you want to buy a boat? Now is certainly the time to talk about that.

And while you're talking, talk, too, about your worries. Will so much togetherness feel confining? Are you afraid that you'll "lose your edge" now that you're leaving the workplace? That you'll feel old or less vital than you are used to? These kinds of fears grow in darkness and silence, but giving them sunlight and air can shrink them down to size. Listen without judging when your partner shares, and stifle the urge to say, "That's silly" or "That won't happen." To the person confessing their fears, they're very real, and you need to respect their feelings even if you don't think their boogeymen are real. Reassure, but don't deny.

Do you expect your spouse to join in with your enthusiasms and new pastimes? They might be eager to do so, on the fence about it, or not remotely interested. In any case, remember this—there's no law that says you have to do everything together just because you're married. I've known couples who took separate vacations because one wanted to tour Thai temples and the other wanted to be in a cabin in the mountains somewhere. And that's absolutely okay—great, in fact, as long as it works for both of you. You choose your own adventures and then come together to share new stories and experiences, both refreshed and renewed. Some couples want to build a vacation home together or even start a small business. Others are happy enjoying their newfound leisure together. It's going to be different for every couple, and the best way to reach some kind of agreement is to talk things out thoroughly and honestly ahead of time. Make lists of things you want to do, places you want to go, experiences you'd like to have, and share them.

Remember, keep an open mind, and don't be afraid to say yes to new things. Life should get bigger, not smaller, when you retire.

Glowing into Your Golden Years

When we make room in our marriage for each of us to have our own interests, the relationship can flourish and grow in new directions. Like the client couple in which the wife loved exotic and challenging travel in far-flung locations, while her spouse wanted to golf at luxury resorts in California, you can expand your horizons as individuals while maintaining a healthy relationship. That couple also took regular trips to visit their kids but also made their personal vacation choices. It takes a lot of trust and confidence in your mate to allow for that kind of freedom, but if you can handle it, it's a real affirmation of your bond. If you like to spring out of bed and go hiking at dawn but your spouse wants to sleep in and hit the spa, you might do better going solo!

If you're the person retiring, don't wade in and start making improvements to the way your spouse has been doing things for years without asking first! You may think she needs a big spice rack right next to the stove, but she may disagree. If she's the primary cook, don't push it. When he retired, my own father wrote up directions for my mother on how she could load the dishwasher more efficiently. She cut him off pretty quickly: "I've been loading it for forty years. If you'd like to take the job over, please feel free—but don't tell me to do it your way when I like my way, just because you're retired."

When we retire, we have time to rekindle the other relationships that the demands of work and family may have caused us to sideline—our friendships. Getting together to do things with old friends, whether that's bowling together or taking a cruise, can be a delightful experience. Not always, of course—particularly if your spouse isn't as compatible with them as you are or doesn't have the same history with the relationship. But for the most part, expanding your social circle makes your world bigger, and that's a good thing. When traveling with other people, it's important to remember that their routines—when they eat dinner, for instance—may not be the same as yours. Same with their choice of activities on vacation. Make room for their choices too. Respect their preferences and look for compromises that will work for you both. This goes a long way to making shared vacations more fun and less like a trudge. Flexibility is important in all our relationships.

We worked with a client couple in which the wife's lifelong dream of retirement had been to leave the city and move out to the country, where she could have a small hobby farm and raise sheep for milk and cheese. The trouble was, she knew nothing about animal husbandry and its challenges or what a big job running a farm is. Her husband wasn't as keen on this idea, to put it mildly. But rather than just saying no, he agreed to explore it with her. They wound up visiting a lot of small farms, talking honestly with the farmers about the workload, and taking some working vacations to learn about the daily demands of animal care. On balance, the wife realized that even hobby farming was a lot more work than she'd imagined and that what might have been a viable choice for their sixties could easily become unmanageable in their seventies, so she decided it wasn't for her. If her husband hadn't taken the time and put in the effort with her to explore her dream and had simply dismissed it out of hand, how might that have impacted their marriage? I'm guessing not well.

Retiring Doesn't Mean Checking Out

Some of us find the idea of going cold turkey from working life daunting because we're just not sure we can deal with going from a fifty-hour workweek to zero. How can we plan for continuing to engage in a productive way with the world now that we're leaving our job?

If this is an issue for you, consider a transition period as a way to ease into retirement rather than just taking the plunge. You might consider working just a couple of days a week, if that's a possibility. Alternatively, you could look around in your area for an interesting volunteer opportunity and commit some regular hours to that. Anything that engages you, offers you out-of-the-house time and gives you some personal space that can help you weather the transition period. We've seen this work wonders for so many people who were intimidated initially by the sudden freedom from schedules and responsibilities retirement brings. And it gives you something fresh to talk about with your partner when you get together.

Lots of couples choose the volunteering route because there are causes dear to their hearts that they'd like to serve. Many times, each member of the couple has their own favorite charity or service organization, so they volunteer separately.

Sometimes one partner is happier spending extended periods with grandkids than the other one is, and that's fine. Rambunctious toddlers or tweens aren't for everyone, and if you love the noise and confusion more than your spouse does, make spending regular time with them your personal commitment. That said, your family relationships need to be handled with care, too, in the shift to different priorities.

Kids and Grandkids—How Retirement Changes the Game

Depending on your children's ages, your retirement can be a big game changer or not so much. Some younger retirees we've worked with have kids who are going through big changes of their own, thanks to puberty or the stresses of teen life. One client told me, "When our daughter hit puberty, it was as though aliens had taken her away and swapped one of their kids into our family. Suddenly she hates us, and everything we say is 'stupid.' The only reason I'm hanging on is that my best friend told me that eventually the aliens would bring her back."

I know for myself that my relationship with my parents got pretty fraught when I was in high school through to about my second year in college. I was argumentative, independent, and impatient with their attempts to talk sense into me. My attitude was not ideal, at least not from their point of view, and I'm sure I caused plenty of friction and hurt feelings. I'm sorry I did, but I'm glad to report that when I matured into a fully functioning adult, my relationship with my folks was transformed and we enjoyed each other's company.

That said, it's easy for parents to forget that their grown-up kids are going to make their own decisions, have their own ideas about child-rearing, and set their own boundaries about how much advice and/or criticism they'll welcome from you. As hard as that can be—they were babies just a minute ago!—you have to listen to and respect those boundaries, because you've done your part raising them. Now you can enjoy a different kind of relationship that is every bit as loving but on a more equal plane.

You're going to like some of their parenting choices and loathe others. You may hate to see your grandkids spending their time on computers or phones or find the way they dress or decorate themselves with hair color, piercings, tattoos, etc. appalling. Why are they fed fast food so often? Shouldn't their grades be better? Or their manners?

Biting your tongue when you want to tell them so is awfully hard, because you've been in the habit of steering your children for many years, and now your beloved grandkids are part of the mix. But before you speak, pause and think, *Would I have appreciated it if my own parents had tried to micromanage my life as an adult?* Probably not. And advice, no matter how well intentioned, can feel like criticism, and nobody wants to hear that.

Instead, offer a caring ear when they choose to confide in you. If advice is asked for, offer it honestly but respectfully. If it's not, don't give it. Remember the old adage: We've got two ears but just one mouth for a reason. Look at this period of your life as an opportunity to have deeper relationships with your adult children. Do your part to keep it on an even keel emotionally, and don't try to take the wheel as they navigate their adulthood.

Different Times, Different Challenges

Sometimes the choices your grandkids make may seem downright odd or even offensive to you. In the past, topics we considered taboo weren't discussed, but contemporary teens feel much more comfortable airing their feelings and choices. Everything is out in the open, on the table, and much more casually discussed than was once the case. You may find this kind of openness refreshing or appalling, depending on your level of flexibility. You may wonder how you're supposed to feel or react to this kind of information. It's undiscovered country for many of us, and it can seem like hostile territory if their choices clash with your ideas of what's right and moral.

But here's the thing. Your grandparents were probably similarly appalled by you when you were a kid. Did you listen to loud rock music, wear tie-dyed clothes, or keep your hair long? Did you burn your bra or protest the war? Maybe you partied hard with your friends and got into some trouble along the way. All these would have seemed outrageous to most of our grandparents, and some of them wouldn't have hesitated to tell us what they thought about where we were headed.

Chances are that your grandkids will do just fine, just as you did and as their parents are doing, by and large. Again, this is probably a time to button your lip and listen. Don't judge; don't dismiss; don't disrespect. This can be tough, but the fact is that those rebellious teens will grow up eventually, and they'll remember who loved them regardless of how they looked or sounded.

Their world is much bigger than ours was, for better or worse. I believe this generation of kids is going to wind up being the best informed we've ever seen, thanks to the internet and the chance to interact on social media. But getting through the teen years is rarely pretty and is fraught with risks, choices, and self-doubt. Most of us come out of it functional and competent, though. Give your grandchildren your love and the space to make their own choices, even their own mistakes, and try not to let the things that are unique to this generation rankle you too much. At the end of the day, you want the relationships to flourish.

Setting Healthy Boundaries

In retirement, it's time to prioritize your own dreams and needs, not to simply trade one kind of work (paid) for another (babysitting, pet sitting, house sitting, etc.). You're not in this world to serve as an ad hoc all-around resource for your kids, certainly not past the point that you want to be or feel comfortable with.

If you live near your adult children and they start leaning on you too much for childcare or anything else, you're going to need to speak up and lay out your limits. For some of us, babysitting young children is just too challenging beyond a certain point. If you're pushed past your limits, you're going to resent it sooner or later, and that's liable to lead to a fight rather than a cool and productive discussion and planning. Don't be afraid to speak up about your own needs. When everyone feels respected and heard, relationships run more smoothly. Set a schedule you can all live with, and you'll enjoy your time together that much more.

Don't plan family vacations without first consulting with all the members you intend to include. What sounds like fun to you may not be as appealing to others or even practical for them. As generous and well intentioned as it can be to plan to take everyone on a cruise together or abroad for the holidays, your adult children and your grandchildren have their own lives and commitments. If you want to plan a family trip, make sure everyone concerned is at the table, and don't get your feelings hurt if your idea of a great trip isn't shared by all. Suggest, listen, and encourage them to weigh in. Don't buy those tickets and stuff them into their Christmas stockings, because they may be more a burden than a gift. For some parents, the idea of traveling with their kids is the opposite of relaxing, even with the grandparents along to help share the work. Respect that, and remember that a good gift is one that's welcomed by the recipient, not the giver.

One area in which many adult children do want and appreciate advice is in how to set themselves up financially for their own retirement. If they ask you for advice, ask them about their goals and tell them how you've managed your own savings and planning over the years. Stop short of reordering their portfolios, but tell them what has worked for you and what hasn't. Helping them achieve financial independence in this way is a great gift.

Bottom Line

Our relationships change during retirement along with everything else! It is possible to keep the romance alive if you're intentional and communicate well. If your marriage is no longer viable for you or your spouse, know that there are many ways to divide and protect your assets and honor your past relationship.

When it comes to your adult children and grandchildren, don't be afraid to prioritize your own activities and goals. Set healthy boundaries and communicate them to children and grandchildren. And remember—you raised your kids. Now let them raise their own.

CHAPTER 8

"Friends—How Do I Keep the Connection?"

"What if I'm lonely?"

"Where will I find friendship without my work 'networks'?"

"How can I balance my 'solitary' time with socializing in retirement?"

Aging brings many challenges to our well-being, including the loss of friends, whether because of ill health, death, a move, or, in the case of retirement, because we no longer see the work friends with whom we spent significant time. Added to that, our long-term friendships may not have been maintained over the years. Keeping these relationships flourishing can be challenging, but it's well worth the effort.

How important is friendship for us as we age? Maybe more important than you realize! Based on a 2019 poll of adults between fifty and eighty, the Institute for Healthcare Policy and Innovation revealed that about 34 percent of people in this group reported feeling lonely, isolated, and/or lacking in social interactions—and that was *before* the pandemic.[3]

How does social isolation affect us? And what are the tangible benefits of friendship—*and the damage that is caused by its absence?* Multiple studies have shown that the impact of loneliness can be devastating and that isolation can either trigger or exacerbate memory loss, depression, and even bad physical health. It's important to note here that withdrawing from friendships and choosing isolation can also be symptomatic of any of these issues, so if you find yourself pulling away from friends in your circle, you might want to see a therapist to talk through that. Of course, there are times we all want to be alone, and that's healthy and normal. But loneliness is neither, so you need to take action to regain your life in society.

In a research paper titled "Friendship in Later Life: A Research Agenda,"[4] authors Rosemary Blieszner, Aaron M. Ogletree, and Rebecca G. Adams, say the following:

> Late-life adults report liking and caring about their friends, laughing together and having fun, feeling satisfied with their relationships, being able to confide in each other, and reminding each other to stay healthy ... Friend ties alleviate loneliness, offer emotional and instrumental support and provide companionship through mutual interests and shared activities ... The feelings of connectedness that these aspects

3 Solway, Erica, et al. "LONELINESS and HEALTH among OLDER ADULTS: RESULTS from the UNIVERSITY of MICHIGAN NATIONAL POLL on HEALTHY AGING." *Innovation in Aging*, vol. 3, no. Supplement 1, Nov. 2019, pp. S600–S601, https://doi.org/10.1093/geroni/igz038.2233. Accessed 9 Jan. 2020.

4 Rosemary Blieszner, Aaron M. Ogletree, and Rebecca G. Adams, "Friendship in Later Life: A Research Agenda," *Innovation in Aging* 3, no. 1 (March 30, 2019): igz005. doi: 10.1093/geroni/igz005. PMID: 30949589; PMCID: PMC6441127.

of friendship convey give meaning to older adults' lives, which is important for well-being. Indeed, exchanging many forms of social support is one of the most important benefits of friendship in the second half of life. The advantages of late adulthood friendship reach beyond psychological well-being. Research shows that relational closeness and social support are also important for maintaining cognitive functioning and physical health in old age.

Stay in Touch with Work Friends

Ideally, when it comes to keeping our work friends, we've had a chance to set up some networks before we exit the job, make some plans, and let the people with whom we want to keep in touch know that they're important to us. Regularly scheduled lunch dates, planned outings to play tennis or golf, or just meeting up for a beer after work on a Friday are ways to keep it casual and keep in touch.

Often when we're retiring, many of the people we've known the longest on the job are also preparing to retire or have recently done so. You can contact those colleagues and set up a lunch date or a trip to the ball game. Getting a regular meetup on the books is a great way to keep friends and break your routine.

You can also choose to mentor your replacement or someone you'd like to see succeed in your old workplace. Most people on their way up would love the chance to bounce ideas off a mentor who could help them understand the culture or challenges specific to their new profession or workplace. As a mentor, you can share the insights and institutional knowledge you've gained through the years and take satisfaction in helping a promising up-and-comer grow their abilities. We know someone who took on the task of creating a mentoring group and contacted former and current execs within his former company to join up and take part. Not only did he and his fellow mentors offer needed wisdom and support; they created a reason to get together and discuss their progress and problems and to organize social events where potential mentors and mentees could meet.

Does your workplace have an alumni club? If so, join up and give it a try. Alumni clubs and reunions, sponsored either by your former school or workplace, can provide opportunities to connect with friends. If your workplace fields a sports team, show up for the games. Many workplaces sponsor employee community outreach efforts via volunteering together for hands-on work, as with Habitat for Humanity, or to raise funds for worthy causes, perhaps by staffing a booth at a local fair or function. Talk to the person who spearheads these initiatives, and ask if you can help. Most often they're happy to have another willing pair of hands.

One of my clients so valued his relationships with local merchants near his former workplace that he'd go out of his way to get his hair cut at the barbershop he'd patronized for years and to have lunch at a nearby diner, too, just to keep up with the people he knew there.

Connecting with Social Media

Social media presents many opportunities to connect and keep up with or rekindle friendships. Consider signing up for Facebook and "following" your workplace's page or the pages of the friends you made there. Your high school graduating class may have a reunion site online, too, which can put you in touch with long-lost classmates. We know folks who have gone on cruises with members of their high school graduating class from fifty years ago and had such a good time they cruised together every year.

Facebook offers all kinds of special interest and hobby groups, too, and no matter what you collect or what activity you enjoy, you're almost certain to find a group dedicated to that very thing. That puts you in touch with others who share your interest and can let you know about conventions, meetings, and swap meets centered around it. If you're looking for a group of local people to walk with or to form a trivia team or kayak with, your town's local Facebook groups would be a good place to post an invitation to connect.

If you can connect on Facebook with old friends from your hometown, high school, or college days, you can see what they've shared about themselves and their current lives and use that as a springboard to get reacquainted. Instagram is another place where people connect, mostly to share photos and short videos.

LinkedIn is another popular option, particularly if you're looking to do some independent consulting work or other part-time employment to ease into retirement. You can keep in touch with work or professional contacts and network with new people who might be able to recommend or use your services. You can also plan meetups and check out conferences or other events coming up in your areas of interest.

How Will a Move Impact Your Friendships?

You and your spouse may have dreamed of leaving your family home behind for somewhere more exotic or suited to a kind of recreation you favor. Maybe you've been looking at a condo on the golf links or are drawing up plans for a beach house on an island somewhere. But when my clients bring up these kinds of big moves, I always ask them if they're moving away from their social networks and if the place they're moving to is likely to offer opportunities to form a new friend group.

One client couple we know were avid skiers and decided to move to a place in the mountains in another state after retirement. It was a beautiful location, but once they were there full time, the remoteness of the location hit them. Not only were they far from their circle of friends, but simple things like going grocery shopping suddenly became a challenge. Heaven forbid you forget to pick up one critical thing, because the whole trip to and from the shopping center took about three hours. Worst of all, even though they loved each other, the demands on their relationship created by this isolation really took a toll on their happiness. They decided to move back to their old neighborhood and kept their dream home for seasonal use, renting it out when they weren't using it.

Whether you're moving to a dream home or to a seniors housing complex, you need to anticipate potentially feeling marooned and lonely at first. If you're part of a couple, that can mitigate it to some extent, but don't put everything on your mate. Find ways to help each other make new connections and find individual activities that work for each of you. Among other things, you'll have something fresh to talk about over dinner.

"Where Can I Meet People?"

We may find ourselves wishing for some new friends, too, but sometimes our friend-making skills seem a little rusty and we're not sure just how to proceed. Here are some ideas for making new connections:

1. *Volunteer for a cause that's meaningful to you.* We'll talk more about this in another chapter, but if you're looking to meet

people motivated by the same values you hold around doing good for your community, there's no better place to start than as a volunteer in an organization. Start slowly—resist the urge to take on too many activities or duties right away. But be a regular attendee at meetings, and take on your share of active efforts. There are all kinds of causes and no shortage of need, so you'll be welcome wherever you offer your help. And by and large, volunteers are about as nice a group of folks as you can find.

2. *Join a group around your interests—or start one!* A retired history professor we know volunteered to run a history reading group at his local library, and it's been going strong for over five years now. There are groups that attend the theater together, who get together to dance (whether that's social dancing, line dancing, clogging, or something in between). There are groups that dedicate time to keeping town parks neat and weeded, groups to support homeless outreach, to work for candidates, to support animal shelters, to staff resale shops that support charities. If you've always wanted to work in the theater, local theater groups offer opportunities to support their efforts, whether by working backstage, as a cast member, or as an usher. Again, don't overcommit, and don't stick yourself with something you're not going to enjoy. There's no shame in trying an activity on and then deciding to move on to another one. Your local senior center probably hosts an array of activities and mixers, and there are online ways to find affinity groups beyond that.
3. *Begin attending religious services or become more active in your church/temple.* You may already know people in a congrega-

tion, or the whole experience may be new to you, but if you're among the faithful, houses of worship offer a place to gather with others and many opportunities to become involved with community or mission efforts. You can go to the after-service coffee hour and talk with your neighbors and fellow congregants. You can help out with rummage sales, meal service for the needy, or other efforts. You can help out in the crying room, sing in the choir, or volunteer to usher or do other regular chores around services. Again, you'll encounter community-minded people who are focused on helping others and will likely be among the most welcoming you'll meet. If your health or other considerations keep you out of congregant situations, there are online opportunities to join discussion groups.

4. *Enroll in continuing education.* Your mind is a terrible thing to waste—so use it. We'll talk more about the benefits of continuing education later, but one of them is certainly that it gives you the chance to gather with other learners and potentially make friends. A scheduled class is a place to be once or multiple times a week, offers the chance to explore areas of interest for you, and helps keep your mind nimble. And the courses can be activity based, like sewing or music, or academic.

5. *Make and accept invitations.* Are you the person whose knee-jerk reaction to being asked out socially is typically no? Alternatively, do you wait for others to make the first move without initiating any invitations to connect? You know who you are, and if either of these describes you, it's time to shake things up.

Start by initiating a social meeting. Pick a person you've been meaning to connect with, and consider what kind of activity is likely to appeal to them and fit into their schedule. Is that lunch? Coffee? Dinner? A movie? Maybe the person likes to hike or walk or bicycle. Maybe you both have dogs and they'd like an outing to a local dog park. The next step is the hardest—actually picking up the phone, sending the text, or firing off the email. If they demur, citing a scheduling conflict, ask them what day or time would work for them. Make the date and keep it. And don't stop with one person; try a second or third. Many people wish for more social connection than they have and would be glad to hear from you. If someone asks you out, go—and use the opportunity to make a follow-up date.

6. *Unattached? Try dating!* If you're flying solo, maybe it's time to change that. A romantic attachment isn't just for the young—it can happen any time if you're available and open to it. If you have someone in sight, use the steps above to initiate that first date, because it certainly isn't going to make itself. If you don't have someone you'd like to know better, ask friends for suggestions or to serve as go-betweens. After all, they know you and are likely to have a good idea about the kind of person you'd do well with. There is also a plethora of online dating services that cater to over sixties, and they're easy to use. SeniorMatch is a great place to begin if you're just dipping your toe into the dating pool. Singles50, eharmony, OkCupid, and OurTime can connect you with other singles in your area. If you're looking for faith-allied dates, Christian Mingle, LDS Singles, or JDate focus on folks whose beliefs align. And if you're intellectually inclined, consider Academic

Singles or EliteSingles. The sites are all easy to use and differ in pricing, so shop around and try one out.

7. *Get fit and meet new people.* That sounds like a win-win, right? You can do it if you join an exercise class or activity group. You'll meet others who are working on their fitness, and having that opportunity to connect can certainly lead to getting together outside class to grab a coffee or a meal. If you're concerned that your fitness level isn't up to snuff, don't be! Gyms are great places to form new friendships, and you almost certainly won't be the only person who doesn't look like a stand-in for Arnold Schwarzenegger. If you're new to the weight room or workout room, don't be afraid to ask people for tips on using the machines correctly. We'll talk more about the importance of good health in the next chapter and how to get from wherever you are to a fitter and happier condition.

Grieving Friendships

Many retirees look forward to spending more time with their old friends, but those well-laid plans can go to pieces when the unexpected happens. Death, serious illness, a move, a divorce—any of these can end a longtime relationship, and the older we get, the more likely we'll lose someone who really matters to us. Grief is a normal part of every phase of life, but for many of us it hits harder when we're already feeling loss and vulnerability because of the changes we're experiencing.

At times like this, the presence of a listening ear is invaluable. That ear can be a family member, a dear friend, a pastor, or a therapist who works with the grieving. If you don't have access to these, consider joining a grief group. These are often run by churches or hospitals and hospice centers. They provide an opportunity to talk about your loss with people who are going through the same things you are.

While it may initially feel odd to be talking about such an intensely felt experience with strangers, it quickly becomes clear that the process of grieving is similar for everyone. Our timetables may differ, but the path from the initial shock and pain to some kind of acceptance is both deeply personal and universal. Talking to and listening to others in similar emotional straits comfort us because we can see that we're not alone.

Grief is a process, and there's no hurrying it along. Find the resources you need to cope and get through it, and don't hesitate to look beyond your circle of friends and family for the support you need.

Consider connecting with the children or other family members of your late friend. They are experiencing grief, too, and getting together to share happy memories of time spent with the missing person can be therapeutic for both of you. They're probably wishing, too, that they had someone to talk to, and you can be one of those people. Get together on your late friend's birthday and have lunch.

When a friend of ours lost her mother, she forged a strong connection with her aunt, who was grieving her sister's loss. The two of them hadn't spent much time together, but each of them saw in the other living reminders of the person they'd lost and were cheered by that. "It was like being with Mom," my friend said, "and my auntie felt the same way about me." They went on cruises, visited regularly, and helped each other past the grieving process.

Be a Regular

Face-to-face interaction is important to us because we're social beings, and the internet, as great a resource as it is, can't substitute for person-to-person contact. Do you remember how discombobulating the COVID-19 lockdowns were, when we all did Zoom meetings and avoided public places? Not surprisingly, that unnatural state of affairs created a wave of mental health issues, particularly among older people and school-age kids. It's certainly not a healthy way to live, so just getting up and watching TV every morning isn't a good option for a healthy retirement.

Going to the workplace every day meant we engaged with others with a common purpose on a regular basis—and that regularity is important. Engagement, energy, and intellectual stimulation were all supplied by our interchanges with our colleagues. When you leave your job, you've got to become proactive in finding other opportunities to get your needed dose of socialization outside your own four walls. Whether it's a local coffee shop, the public library, or a senior center, it's great to have a place that's a regular stop for you, somewhere you'll reliably see familiar faces and find people to talk to. A gym can provide that kind of contact, too, and comes with the added benefit of contributing to your wellness.

A good friend of ours found his "social spot" on a bench downtown in the small town where he lives. Every morning he'd sit there to read his newspaper and have his coffee. One day he struck up a conversation with another guy who had the same routine. A third man, a friend of the second fellow, stopped by to chat, then a fourth, and in no time this bench became a daily stop every morning for all four of them where they'd chew over the news of the day, share their life philosophies, and wish all politicians to a hot place. Without meaning to, our friend had become a regular, and he looked forward to that daily hour and missed it on days when the weather or other obligations made attendance impossible.

Your circle of regulars may be people you don't see elsewhere, like the group you have lunch with once a week at a senior center or the folks you meet up with to walk the mall circuit. But that's the beauty of it. Ideally, we've got multiple circles of acquaintances in our lives: family, longtime friends, colleagues or former colleagues we see occasionally, and folks we may see once a year or so when there's a big gathering. But just having someone to exchange pleasantries with is a great way to keep you engaged in the world, and that's good for your health.

"My Spouse Takes Care of All That Social Stuff"

Opposites attract, and very often a couple is made up of one extrovert and one introvert. The extrovert is the one initiating social contact and making dates for both of them to go to dinner or parties or family gatherings. Very often this role falls to the wife, and the husband more or less goes along with her planning. He gets the benefits of socialization without having to make the effort, and everyone is happy. But when you're the less outgoing one and something happens to your extroverted partner, your social life can evaporate and you may find yourself alone too much, even if you hadn't seen yourself as a person who needs others.

How do you cope with your loss and the subsequent feelings of isolation?

- *Start with accepting invitations, as hard as that may be.* People mean well, and as awkward as you might feel being out in the world without your mate, it's something you need to begin to get comfortable with. Old friends understand better than most what you've lost and can help you start to find some balance in your life at a point when it's been knocked askew. Nobody expects you to be "all better" or the life of the party, because they know what you're experiencing.
- *Find ways to celebrate your lost loved one's life by taking up a cause or a group they'd supported.* Arnie's wife loved dogs and volunteered at a local animal shelter. When she passed away, he became a pet "foster parent" who took dogs awaiting adoption into his home on weekends to keep them socialized and help train them. Walking his various foster pets, he found himself interacting with neighbors and others along the way and making plans to meet up for walks or doggie playtime. It got him out of the house and into the habit of talking to people again.
- *Consider therapy.* I know I've extolled the value of the therapeutic relationship elsewhere in this book, but I also understand that for a more introverted individual, the idea of sharing intimate feelings and being vulnerable with a stranger can be anathema. But the thing is, grief and stress are hard on us, not only emotionally but physically too. Talking can provide some release and relief, and we may be self-conscious about oversharing with friends or family. If you had a heart condition, would you feel it was a sign of weakness to see a cardiologist? Probably not. Consider a therapist as the cardiologist for your emotional heart, and give it a try. It takes a while to build a relationship

with a therapist, but it's worth the effort, and the sense it gives you of moving forward in your life is valuable to your healing.

- *Take a part-time job.* What interests you? What skills do you have to share? Even if you don't need the money, a part-time job can give you a way to share your knowledge and talk to people regularly. Hal is a client of ours who was an avid DIYer and over the years had accumulated an impressive breadth of knowledge about how to fix things. He'd spent many Saturday afternoons browsing at his local hardware store, chatting with the clerks and familiarizing himself with the store's stock. When he lost his wife, he needed something to do and somewhere to be—and when he saw a notice in the hardware store's window advertising for part-time help, he went for it. Now he's there every weekend and really enjoys helping others with advice on their home projects. Another client had been a formidable tennis player in her youth and won a lot of country club trophies over the years. She saw a chance to share what she knew with children via her town's park and recreation summer programs and is enriching their lives as much as her own.
- *It's never too late to learn the skills of what we call "charm."* What makes people appealing to others? Most often when you analyze it, it's how good they make others feel about themselves, not how well they themselves appear. Introverts are often uncomfortable with talking about themselves but can certainly practice their conversational skills by learning to lead the other person to talk. Most folks like to talk about themselves; learn to ask questions that draw them out on their favorite topics. Do they have pets? Grandchildren? Where do they like to vacation? Listen to the answers, and follow up to show that you're inter-

ested. Maintain eye contact and let your body language mirror your conversational partner's. The essence of charm is in fact making the other person feel fascinating.

Bottom Line

We are social animals, and friendships are vital to our well-being at every stage of our lives. Make building and maintaining relationships a priority and part of your self-care. It's as essential as exercise and intellectual stimulation, so even if you're naturally shy, look for ways to increase your interactions with the world.

CHAPTER 9

Taking Care of Body and Mind

Bad news, folks. Retirement can be hard on your health.

An often-cited 2011 study[5] discovered the following:

> It is found that retirement significantly increases the risk of being diagnosed with a chronic condition. In particular, it raises the risk of a severe cardiovascular disease and cancer. This is also reflected in increased risk factors (e.g., BMI, cholesterol, blood pressure) and increased problems in physical activities. Furthermore, retirement worsens self-assessed health and an underlying health stock.

It would be easy for us to shrug this off as simply evidence of diminishing physical returns as we age, but this isn't a case of causation equaling correlation, because data also shows that seventy-year-olds who continue working have *fewer* heart attacks and cancer than their retired same-age peers. A 2015 study of eighty-three thousand older adults over fifteen years, published in the CDC journal *Preventing*

5 Stefanie Behncke, "Does Retirement Trigger Ill Health?" *Health Economics* 21, no. 3 (March 2012): 282–300, https://doi.org/10.1002/hec.1712.

Chronic Disease, suggested that people who worked past age sixty-five were about three times more likely to report being in good health and about half as likely to have serious health problems such as cancer or heart disease than did their retired peers.[6]

Put aside the appalling cosmic injustice of this—how is it fair that after all your hard work, your health deserts you when you retire?—*why* does this happen, and what can we do to prevent our health from taking a hit when we leave our jobs behind?

Activity, both physical and mental, is the key to preserving a healthy body and healthy mind. Work provides us with intellectual, social, and, usually to some degree, physical activity. It keeps us alert and interacting with others. We have to get up, dress, and leave the house to get there, so we're on a regular schedule. Our jobs may be active or deskbound, but they keep us engaged.

In a study published in 2009,[7] the authors asserted the following:

> Moderate but regular physical activity is associated with a reduction in total mortality among older people, a positive effect on primary prevention of coronary heart disease and a significant benefit on the lipid profile. Improving body composition with a reduction in fat mass, reducing blood pressure and prevention of stroke, as well as type 2 diabetes, are also well established. Prevention of some cancers (especially that of breast and colon), increasing bone density and prevention of falls are also reported. Moreover, some longi-

6 Kachan, Diana, et al. "Health Status of Older US Workers and Nonworkers, National Health Interview Survey, 1997–2011." *Preventing Chronic Disease*, vol. 12, 24 Sept. 2015, https://doi.org/10.5888/pcd12.150040. Accessed 2 Apr. 2020.

7 T. Vogel, P.-H. Brechat, P.-M. Leprêtre, G. Kaltenbach, M. Berthel, and J. Lonsdorfer, "Health Benefits of Physical Activity in Older Patients: A Review," *International Journal of Clinical Practice* 63, no. 2 (March 2009): 303–20. doi: 10.1111/j.1742-1241.2008.01957.x. PMID: 19196369.

tudinal studies suggest that physical activity is linked to a reduced risk of developing dementia and Alzheimer's disease in particular.

While many of us look to our parents' lifespans as reliable predictors of our longevity, thanks to advances in medicine and pharmacology we're likely to live longer than our parents did. That means that if we don't take steps to preserve our wellness, we're likely to live longer but be in poorer health. That's not an attractive prospect. So, do we have to stay in harness if we want longer and healthier lives?

No, we do not. There's a lot we can do to mitigate that risk and support a healthier and more active old age. If you can stay focused, stay active, and stay scheduled and on a regular routine, you can support your wellness and enjoy life longer.

Let me tell you about Pete, a client in his eighties who lives down on the coast toward Corpus Christi. We just love to talk with him because every time we check in with him, he regales us with stories of surfing and fierce pickleball tournaments. He's in the ocean and on the court multiple times a week, and he is loving life. He's been hit with some rough challenges, like the loss of his spouse and of an adult child to cancer. But he didn't let these things derail him. He continued to practice his wellness routine, and it supported his body and spirit. His optimistic outlook prevails, and he enjoys every day.

It's Not Too Late

When's the best time to start a fitness routine?

Today.

Pete didn't really start daily exercise until the day after he retired—and the word *routine* is critical to why he's enjoyed such a happy, healthy old age. He's free of most of the aches and pains that trouble his contemporaries thanks to his commitment to daily exercise.

Why does routine matter so much? Because unlike so many things that dictate our quality of life, habits are within our control. We can make them, and we can change them. Building a new habit takes about two months of repetition before it sticks. Once you've committed to it for that long, you'll feel uncomfortable when you miss it. Are you willing to commit to two months if you know it will improve your health and quality of life?

So many of us spend our careers tied to our desks. Long days at work leave us tired and wanting nothing more than to plop down in our favorite chair and do nothing much, apart from watching a little TV or cruising the internet. Maybe we get out to play golf on the weekends or mow the lawn, but that's about it. Then, when we retire, that chair looks awfully welcoming, and what had been our evening routine turns into our all-day routine. And that is literally deadly.

You're at the start of a new chapter in your life. You can make whatever you want of it. Why not make it active?

Old age brings a lot of new challenges to our health—arthritis, aches and pains, issues with blood pressure, problems with vision and hearing, and more. But pushing back against decline is possible, and once you acquire that healthy routine, you'll not only feel better; you'll also feel better about yourself.

So how do you get started? The first step is a checkup visit with your doctor. Tell them what it is you're hoping to achieve. If you've got limitations, they'll tell you how to safely work within them. If there are underlying health issues that need to be addressed before you start, this is the time to take care of them. It's important to be realistic about goals, because incremental improvement is the only sensible way to approach exercise. Pushing past your limits and challenging yourself to go further sounds great in the context of a sporting goods ad, but in real life, if you've been largely sedentary, it's a recipe for injury or worse.

Be smart as you step into this new experience. Which of us has not at some point started a diet or decided to take up an active habit like running, gone hard at it for a week (or a day), and found ourselves nursing a mean case of shin splints after a run that we weren't physically prepared for—or eating a sack of cookies that were supposed to be for the grandkids?

If you get impatient, remember—it took you a long time to get to this point, and it will take a while to get back to where you want to be. The good news is that if you stick with it, you'll see real improvement in a few months. After a year, you'll feel younger than you did on your last birthday.

"How Do I Get Fit?"

What did the man say when asked how he ate an elephant? "One bite at a time." The journey from a sedentary lifestyle to a healthy one is best accomplished with small steps. Look at your daily routine, and find a time in your day you can commit to taking that first small step.

- *A twenty-minute walk every morning or afternoon is a great way to start.* Get yourself a pair of good-fitting walking sneakers, and put it on your calendar. Let your spouse know not to make plans at that time for the pair of you, or better yet, invite them to join you. If you're walking alone, treat yourself to some earbuds and find something to listen to. That could be a lively playlist of music that inspires you to move or an audible book or podcast you're interested in. The important thing is the scheduling and the regularity. For some folks, getting a dog provides both the schedule and the reason for walking, because a dog won't take "Not today" for an answer.

- *Sign up for a class through your local parks and recreation association or at a gym.* Don't jump straight into boot camp—look for starter classes that encourage movement and increase mobility. Yoga, aquacise, beginning strength training, or even Zumba are all good fits for a beginner, because you can do as much as you can without pushing harder than you should. Talk to the instructor before you start, tell them where you are in your fitness journey, and listen to their recommendations regarding how much to do. The point is to make yourself stronger, not knock yourself out. It's a marathon, not a sprint, so pace yourself. Progress will come.
- *Consider joining a gym* and commit to going there for a minimum of three days a week for an hour. Find a gym where you can get some advice on fitness and where a qualified trainer can help you plan a routine and learn to use the equipment safely and effectively. If you don't have the right clothes—stretchy and moisture-wicking fabrics are ideal—get some, along with the right shoes. You'll find more than exercise opportunities there; gyms are a great way to socialize if you want to expand your circle of friends, and it's very easy to ask someone who's clearly a regular the right way to use a particular machine or to spot you if you're lifting.
- *Take on a personal trainer.* It may sound like an extravagance, but many gyms offer trainers' services for very reasonable fees, and the payback on that investment is tremendous for you. So many of us go off the rails early on in the habit-building process because we don't have the support and accountability

a trainer supplies. The high-tech workout machines can be intimidating at first sight, and we literally don't know where to start. All that is eliminated with a good trainer, who will explain how to use them correctly, teach you how to stretch before and after a workout, and help you to develop a routine addressed specifically to your needs and limitations, if any. If you've not been in the habit of exercise before, a trainer gets you past the uncertainty and helps you toward becoming a "regular." Three times a week is a great way to start, because it's often enough to make an impact without impinging too much on your time.

How big a difference can it make? One client told me that she'd felt like she was literally dying in her easy chair after a few months of retirement. A self-described klutz, she'd always been embarrassed by her appearance and had successfully avoided gyms since she'd graduated from high school. But the sense of rapid falling away of her health and strength scared her into trying something new, and she elected to splurge on a trainer. She credits that choice with saving her life and says three years on that she's fitter and more mobile now than she was back then. She told me, "I'm aging backward!" and credits her trainer with making it possible. They've become good friends, too, which was an unlooked-for added benefit.

- *Fitness doesn't have to mean drudgery.* If you enjoy an activity, you're more likely to repeat it. Dance classes for adult beginners, walking daily with a friend group, or taking up an active sport like hiking, basketball, racquetball, or pickleball are all great ways to bring some fun to your fitness quest.

- *Keep a fitness journal.* How many reps of a particular exercise did you accomplish today? How many laps did you swim, or how many miles did you put on your walking shoes? You'll be reminded of your progress and how well you're doing when you reread older entries, and you'll be that much prouder of your success as you go along.
- *Find a fitness partner.* This can be your spouse, a friend, or a retired colleague you'd like to stay in touch with. Maybe you want someone to play a sport with, take walks with, or go to a class with. This can be someone you can meet at the gym and work out with or someone you hike or walk your dog with. It adds a social element to what might otherwise feel like a solitary pursuit and, again, brings accountability into the mix for both of you.

  One of our clients loved golf and looked forward to playing daily when he retired. His wife was primarily a homemaker and hadn't ever golfed, but as his retirement got closer, she decided she'd take it up so she could enjoy it with him. She wasn't sure she'd like it, but she was willing to try, so she signed up for golf lessons. To everyone's surprise, she loved it and became a better golfer than he was! She met a whole new circle of friends and started playing regularly in a league. He had a bunch of golf buddies in a different league, and once he retired, they both played all the time, planning their vacations around great golf courses. It's really been great for both of them—and for their fitness.

Fitness Can Help You Through Transitions

Changes in our lives are inevitable, but as we see with Pete, how we face them and the attitude we bring can make a huge difference in how well we cope with them.

One of our clients was a lovely woman whose husband, Paul, became ill and who faithfully cared for him during his years-long decline up through hospice. The hard work and stress of it all nearly ruined her health, and when he finally passed, she looked and felt years older than she was. She could have resigned herself to that but chose instead to put the same love and energy into self-care as she'd put into caring for her spouse. She started going to the gym every other day, walking every morning, and getting counseling for weight loss. Little by little, she pulled herself back from the brink and regained her health. She still missed her husband, but this goal provided a positive, proactive way to address grief in a way that supported her wellness, both mental and physical. Within a couple of years, she was almost unrecognizable. When she talked about it, she told me, "Paul would have been so proud of me!"

Maintaining Baseline Health

When we're working, it's too easy to put off the routine maintenance that goes with looking after our bodies. Don't we all know someone who's never missed a scheduled oil change on his beloved car but hasn't been to the doctor for years because "If it ain't broke, don't fix it"? So many things can be fixed if they're caught early on, and too many of them can cause serious or even fatal illness if left unchecked.

If you haven't had a physical in more than a year, do yourself and your loved ones a favor and get it done. If you've not had a colonoscopy or haven't had one in years, get it done if your doctor says you should. If you've not had blood work done, or if you've got an issue that's causing you irritation, but not enough to drive you to make a doctor's appointment, pick up the phone and make an appointment. Is there a history of heart disease, cancer, diabetes, etc. in your family? Tell your doctors about that so they know where to be extra vigilant. Submit to the tests, follow up with the specialists if your primary care doctor feels you need to do so, and minimize your risks. A seemingly minor issue—frequent headaches, for instance, or a digestion issue—can signal something much more significant and really shouldn't be relegated to the "ain't broke…" pile.

We know that some issues can be scary to confront and that it might seem easier to simply let them go and hope they improve. But that's a lot to put on luck, and if you suspect that your memory is less reliable than it ought to be or that the pain in your side that just doesn't go away might be something you need to worry about, gather up your courage and go see the doctor. If there's no problem, tests will tell you so. And if there is, early detection is your best defense.

Don't forget that regular check-in with your optometrist. Sometimes something like cataracts can fade our vision so slowly that we're only aware of how badly we see when we're trying to drive at night. Many degenerative eye conditions can be diagnosed and treated successfully if they're caught early.

And if your hearing isn't what it used to be, visit an audiologist. If you find yourself turning up the TV or radio all the time or missing what's being said to you, you should know that the technology to support your hearing is an area of medical research that has improved exponentially over the past decade. These aren't your grandparents' hearing aids, and if you find out you need them, you'll be amazed to hear all you've been missing. Hearing loss is a problem many of us face in later life, and the self-consciousness it can create often causes a person to fall away from social life and become isolated. Don't let that happen to you. Added to this, your brain has to go into overdrive trying to hear and decipher what you're missing, which is exhausting! Getting your hearing restored will make you feel better and more in touch with the world around you.

Another aspect of health we don't think of as often as we should is our oral health. Make sure you're getting your regular visits to the dentist in, along with scheduling the cleanings and repairs you need. Your oral health has a big impact on your overall physical well-being, so don't neglect it. Your exam can uncover other kinds of issues beyond a cracked tooth or failing filling, things like grinding or oral cancer, for instance. It's a small investment of time that pays big dividends for your health.

Expect the Unexpected—and Plan Ahead

People are living longer but also having to manage longer periods of living with poor health. Diseases that used to kill folks in prior decades are mercifully no longer lethal, but they often do require significant time and funds to manage. As we age, we're liable to get sidelined by illness or injuries that wouldn't have worried us in our youth. I know we've talked about this in previous chapters, but in the light of maintaining wellness, let's touch on it again. *It matters where you live* and what kind of help will be available to you in the event you need it. The older you get, the more critical location can be. Take this into consideration if you're thinking about moving, particularly if you're eyeing somewhere that's far outside your circle of friends, family, and trusted medical professionals.

A remote cabin on a mountainside is a lovely place to be—unless you have a heart attack. How long will it take to get an ambulance? How long if your partner gets you into the car and drives you to the hospital—assuming, of course, they are able to carry you, because you're not likely to be able to walk. The same can be true for small towns or rural areas both across the United States and abroad, where hospitals may be few and far between.

The quality of care you can expect at your local hospital is also very important, and it's worth the effort to do the research out ahead of need, certainly before house hunting. Check out their ratings and what their specialties are. If you've got renal issues, will you need dialysis at some point? Dialysis centers can be hard to get to depending on your location, so again, plan ahead. Finding good doctors who are accepting new patients isn't as easy as it once was, particularly in the middle of the country, so dig into lists of practitioners and see whose reviews and background matches up with your needs. If you're among those fortunate enough to continue to enjoy health insurance benefits from your employer after retirement, call the insurer and find out whether those benefits will travel with you outside city or state lines or national boundaries.

Have you got family members within easy driving distance? Should you need help because of a health issue, that's going to be important. Having a circle of friends you can call on if you need to provides peace of mind.

Long-term care insurance is no longer widely available, and unless you signed up for it at age fifty or so, it's unlikely you can get it for a reasonable price. This is a bigger issue for couples, because if one of you goes into a long-term care facility and the other stays in the family home, you're now paying two sets of living expenses. A single person is trading one set of expenses for another, so it's not as onerous.

If you get to a point at which you need regular assistance with the daily activities of living, you're probably going to need to hire someone to come to your home. Many of our clients worry about that expense, but in budgeting against that need, remember that your discretionary spending will go down. Consider, too, a move to a retirement community that offers options for home care, housekeeping, and on-site skilled nursing care. These can vary wildly in price depending on where you live but offer real peace of mind if you or your partner is clearly going to need more assistance down the line. Do shop around and personally visit any facility you're considering. One client told me that her father, who had dementia, had to be put in a special care facility when she could no longer manage him safely at home. Where she lived, the cost for his care was $14,000 per month, which was unaffordable for them. She found a nicer place in the small Midwest town where his extended family lived for $6,000 a month.

Little Things That Mean a Lot

Small actions can contribute in a big way to our physical and mental health:

1. *Stay hydrated.* If you don't already carry a water bottle with you, get one and make it a habit. Dehydration is all too common among older folks, and even mild dehydration can cause problems with blood pressure, heart rate, and body temperature. If you're feeling tired, try drinking more water.
2. *Sleep disturbances are a big contributor to ill health.* If you find you've become a noisy snorer, or if you regularly wake

up in the small hours and can't get back to sleep, talk to your doctor. Establishing good sleep hygiene and a regular routine around bedtime can help. Resist the temptation to scroll through your phone. Alcohol consumption, heavy meals before bedtime, and caffeine late in the day can all cause wakefulness. Regular daily exercise can help you rest better at night, but avoid workouts within three hours of hitting the hay.

3. *Stay away from Debbie or Don Downer*—that acquaintance or neighbor who just can't stop complaining about everything. Whether it's politics, health, or the state of the world in general, this person sees nothing but the downside. That kind of mindset can be contagious, so limit your exposure to them. Focus on the positive as much as you can, and if you hear yourself complaining, make a conscious effort to turn your thoughts in a brighter direction.

4. *Make sure you're eating right and having regular meals,* not just grabbing whatever is at the front of the fridge. When we retire, our eating habits change. The snacking habit can pack on pounds and usually leads us to eat more processed foods, more carbs, more salt, and more sugar than we ought to. If your work diet wasn't reliably healthful, now is your chance to establish better habits. Try a food diary for a week; just jot down what you eat every day, down to the last cookie, and review it at the end of the week with good nutrition in mind. Do you see any patterns in the choices you're making that you might change for the better with a more mindful approach? Now's not the time to let your body down, because it will let you down if you do.

5. *Keep your mind fit by trying new things.* Learn a language; there are multiple apps like Duolingo and Babbel available for your smartphone, and you can find low-fee or free language learning groups at libraries and senior centers too. Some people enjoy becoming literacy volunteers, helping nonnative English speakers gain fluency while getting to practice another language with a native speaker. And if you really want to absorb a new language in a hurry, nothing works better than an immersion course, where you speak the new language for weeks at a time and are surrounded by native speakers.

Bottom Line

As you age, your health is ever more important, and you've got to be a good steward of your wellness. If your physical and mental fitness haven't been something you've worked at in the past, now's the best time to change that mindset and get in shape. Investments made in your wellness now will help you age with more strength, mobility, and energy, so don't hesitate to join that gym, buy those walking shoes, or change the way you eat. You're worth it.

Similarly, don't put off deferred maintenance on your body. Get that physical, go for the eye or hearing tests you've been putting off, and schedule a trip to the dentist.

Look ahead and start considering what your options will be if and when you need more help, either at home or in an assisted-living community.

CHAPTER 10

"How Will I Stay Busy?"

"How can I afford vacations and travel during retirement?"

"How can I balance having fun with learning and growing?"

"How do I budget to explore new hobbies without breaking the bank?"

Leisure time is a wonderful thing. We spend our working lives looking forward to weekends and vacations, heading back to work when they're over to daydream about how we'll spend our retirement. But when we lose the structure of a working life, we're on our own—and there's a limit to how much hammock time we really want. How can we stay busy, enrich our lives, and embrace new interests?

Two *Wall Street Journal* reporters interviewed a group of retirees about what errors they'd made in planning for retirement.[8] Here is what they reported:

> Many retirees say they realized too late how they could have prepared for a more financially secure and rewarding post-work life. They would have focused on saving more money to cover the higher cost of living. Or they would have put more time into building relationships, taking better care of their health or cultivating new pursuits …
>
> Jim Pilzner, a retired entrepreneur, regrets not setting goals for himself when he retired about four years ago. Now 78, he found there is only so much golf to play and only so many lunches to go to. "I would counsel my younger self, and any other active, achieving person to recognize what drives them and what success really means," said Pilzner. Jim Pilzner is pursuing a degree in political science and history at 78. He eventually figured out that the two things that motivated him most during his career—taking action and learning new things—were the same recipe he needed for retirement.

Retirement done right isn't the end of something as much as it is a new beginning—a personal declaration of independence, if you will. Now we call our own shots, responsibilities, or working schedules.

But we don't change our stripes as easily as we change our titles. If you're a leader, you're going to be looking for a cause and people to lead. If you're project driven and accomplishment oriented, you're going to be looking for things to get done. If you've poured your life into the mastery of a profession, whether that's dentistry or home

---

8 Veronica Daghar and Anne Tergesen, "How to Retire Better, from Retirees Who Learned the Hard Way," *Wall Street Journal*, September 24, 2023.

building, you may feel as though you're leaving behind the most productive part of yourself when you retire.

How can you avoid or mitigate this disconnect? As does the gentleman quoted above, you need to know yourself well enough to understand what keeps you engaged with life and the world and look for ways to integrate that kind of activity into your retirement life. For myself, I know that my vacations are always active rather than restful. I'm looking for adventure, new experiences, and challenges, and while I may take a nap in a hammock, it's a pause, not a goal. Even if you're more inclined to read about adventures than you are to have them, you're still going to need reasons to get up and out of your chair, because when leisure becomes the norm, you're going to want to break it up with activity. Some of us have concrete goals and plans in place for how we'll launch into our new lives, while others are mostly winging it. Either way can work if you keep an open mind and are flexible enough to change things up should the way you're going no longer appeal to you.

Easing into Retirement

In that first year after retirement, you may feel at odds with yourself and hanker for a defined direction without knowing exactly what it should be. Here's what we tell our clients: If you've been contemplating a big project—renovating your home or building a cabin, for instance—this first postretirement year is a great opportunity to get it done. You've got the energy, you've got the time, and you'll have that much longer to enjoy the fruits of your improvement efforts if you go ahead with your project now. Working with an architect, designer, or builder gives you an opportunity to get creative and make sure your ideas are incorporated into the finished project. Without a work schedule, you don't have to hand the reins entirely to someone else. You've got the time to think it through, do the research on what's available and what others have done, and really make it your own. A big project is a reason to get up and get going every morning.

We had some clients who bought a property with a small home on it before they retired. Leading up to retirement, they had done a lot of the planning for the dream home they wanted to put on this property, and for them that became a hobby in itself—going to home shows, crunching the numbers, choosing the finishes. The wife retired a year ahead of her husband, but he was able to work from home during that time, and they effectively became their own general contractors. Not everyone is up to that level of involvement, but in their process of preparation, they'd done a lot of research on what the job required, so they were prepared. It took all of two years to complete it down to the fencing and landscaping, though they moved in before the last of the finishing touches were done. It was a great way to kick off their new lives together and to renew their bond as a couple. Every time we talk to them, they're still upgrading and adding finishing touches. They bought a couple of dogs to round out their new rural life, and they couldn't be more thrilled with it all. They're still just a couple of hours outside the city, so they're able to get in and do things when they choose to.

Not everyone wants to take on a project on that scale, of course. Some of us love to attack the little jobs that have been piling up because we've been too busy to tackle them, and they can be as satisfying but cost a lot less. These could be everything from cleaning out closets and redoing the kids' bedrooms into guest rooms to finishing the attic as a hobby room. Maybe your deferred project is weeding out the gardens, organizing the Tupperware drawer, cleaning out the junk drawers, or donating a lot of books you've already read or don't plan to. There's satisfaction to be found in bringing order out of chaos and getting yourself and your living space squared away to enter this new phase in life.

The Joys of Travel

Travel—whether exotic and adventurous or a cross-country road trip in an RV—is a longtime dream for many retirees we know. Some have planned and budgeted for their big trips for years, while others have confined their preparations to marking up travel books and making lists of destinations. Whatever your style and preferences, it pays to include some discretionary expenses in the budget, because travel and leisure need to be accounted for. It's likely that in some years you're going to take bigger trips, whether you wish to celebrate an anniversary, your kid decides to get married out of town, or you want to attend your high school reunion. You'll feel more comfortable doing these things if they don't require you to break the piggy bank to fund them. The market's performance can certainly impact the timing of trips that aren't tied to a specific date, and when it's up and you can take profits, this can be the ideal time to go ahead and take that safari. It's not going to happen every year, but it's a bonus when it does, and it helps you avoid dipping into your nest egg. If your budget says you can afford to spend $10,000, you need to think it through, though, because you've got to keep inflation in mind when you're planning discretionary spending. That said, most of us don't spend that "mad money" every year, so we stay within our big-picture budgets when we do splurge.

To get the most out of your big trips, invest in something that will help you save money and get more for what you do spend; advance planning costs nothing but your time, and for many people it's a huge part of the fun of travel. There are almost always multiple paths to where you want to go and what you want to do. And advance planning means you can take advantage of savings during, say, an airline ticket price war or special pricing on tours or cruises. Using the time to map out an itinerary lets you figure out the costs of in-country travel and make choices that combine convenience with price. It also allows you to spread out payments over time for a big-ticket item like a cruise or tour.

The way in which you pay matters too. If you love travel, it's probably smart to consider using a credit card that rewards you with miles you can use on airlines, hotels, etc. to help defray your costs. Are you good about reliably paying your credit cards off in a timely fashion? Switch to a card with a solid rewards program and competitive costs, and use it for everything. That may sound counterintuitive if you've been taught that credit cards are dangerous, but it's actually safer to use it for bills as long as you pay your balance off on time. It makes it easier to track your expenses, which can be helpful both in budgeting and at tax time. Avoid using it if there's a cost to you, as there usually is if you use it to pay, for instance, your real estate taxes.

Some cards offer double or triple points for travel spending or restaurants; some give you double points if you book your travel through them directly. If you've done your research on flights and chosen the one you want, you can call the credit card rewards travel department, and they can book it for you using your enhanced miles as payment.

Want Bargains? Be Flexible!

In high seasons for travel, typically summers and during school breaks, you're going to pay more to go places and see things. But now that you're retired, unless you want to take your grandchildren with you,

you can plan your trips for the shoulder seasons like spring or fall or the offseason (normally winter, apart from skiing destinations). Airfare will generally be less expensive, as will hotels, and you'll have more choices available. It's less fun to visit a place when the streets are packed with other tourists and every attraction has a line to get in. Out of season, you can experience something much more like the locals do, at a less hurried pace and with fewer crowds to contend with. Of course, some cities are year-round tourist destinations that don't really have an offseason in terms of visitors; Venice and Florence in Italy always seem to be shoulder to shoulder with people. But for the most part, your dollars will go further and your choices will be greater in the shoulder seasons, so do some comparison shopping. Don't neglect to do your research on typical weather and temperatures, too, since you probably don't want to be in Bangkok during the hot season or up to your neck in snow in the Sierras.

Cruises, too, can be better bargains in the offseasons. Do your cruise research carefully if you're a neophyte, because the different cruise lines have very distinct personalities in terms of the atmosphere on board and the kinds of people who go on them. If you want to get away from shrieking kids, you're probably better off not going with Disney and choosing an adults-only cruise. If you like a lot of shore excursions and some erudition along the way, there are several companies that offer river cruises, mostly in Europe or along the Nile, where you can fill your days with guided sightseeing and your evenings with expert lectures on the history, architecture, and cuisines of the places you're visiting.

If you've always wanted to circumnavigate the globe, there are cruises for that. If you want to sail rather than steam, many cruises offer that kind of experience. If you don't mind a less event-packed schedule on board and prefer fewer fellow cruisers, you can find bargains on repositioning cruises. There are multiple sites online where you can look at different cruise options and compare prices, schedules, and reviews. Again, you're in the catbird seat, because your schedule isn't dictated by work or school calendars, so you can pay less and avoid crowds.

If you belong to a membership warehouse store like Costco, check their travel and tour sales. Very often you'll find that they offer more free extras and better pricing on cruises, tours, and car rentals than you can find elsewhere.

Consider Short-Term Rentals

If you want to go somewhere and stay awhile, you may find you need things that hotels typically don't provide—at least, not at no or low cost—like a place to do laundry or a fully equipped kitchen where you can prepare meals. You've probably heard of or tried rental agencies like Airbnb and Vrbo that connect homeowners with vacationers looking for the comfort and convenience of home without a long-term commitment. These can be excellent resources, particularly if you want to stay somewhere for a week or longer, because they're often no more expensive than hotels. That said, if you're going to book one of these, it's important that you put in the time to research a number of things about your location before renting.

First, if you're renting in an unfamiliar area, you need to know what kind of neighborhood you're booking yourself into. If you're going to a big city, this can make the difference between feeling and being safe or not, so read up on what areas are more central and have a lower crime rate, and spend a little more to stay in them. A bargain isn't worth much if you have to worry about getting mugged when you step out for dinner. Look at maps of public transportation in the area you want to visit; is it readily available and close by your rental? Can you walk to most of the attractions you want to see? If not, you'll find yourself taking cabs or renting a car, and you can burn through a lot of money that way without getting much in return.

Second, when you go on the agency's website, take the time to look at every available rental in the areas you've chosen, and compare what's offered. Be sure to check out things that might be make-or-break items for you. How many beds does it have, and what size are they? How many flights of stairs can you manage? If the answer is none, make sure the places you're considering have elevators. Is there a washer and a dryer? Many Europeans don't have dryers and hang their clothes out to dry, so short-term rentals will often have only washers available. Depending on the weather, hanging your clothes out to dry might be an issue, so read carefully. If the place is centrally located, you may have to deal with street noise, so be prepared for that.

Third, read the reviews *very* carefully—and don't go with anything having a lower than 4.7-star average. People tend to be quite generous in reviewing these places, but if you read carefully, you can usually ferret out the issues others might have had, either with the landlord or the rental itself. Check, too, to make sure the reviews are up to date. If nobody has reviewed a place in a year, there may be an issue. If there are fewer than twenty reviews, move on.

Fourth, read the owner's profile. What other properties do they own or manage? What are the reviews on those? Read them too.

Last, read the terms of your rental before you rent. What's expected of you as the renter? Must you clean the place yourself before you leave? What are the cancellation and refund policies? These differ widely from place to place, so make sure you've read them thoroughly. Do reviews mention that the home was difficult to access or that the landlord wasn't easy to contact or helpful? What amenities are provided? Know, too, that you can sometimes negotiate a better price if you're planning on staying longer than a week or two, so don't be afraid to ask.

Every landlord is different, and some can certainly be problematic, so don't dismiss any red flags. If the landlord contacts you directly and suggests you pay them rather than the agency to book, don't do it. There's no protection for you under those circumstances, and some landlords use that as a way to avoid getting reviewed.

Traveling Solo? You're Not Alone

We may want to take a trip that doesn't interest our partner, or we may be without a partner. Traveling alone can be daunting, particularly to unfamiliar places, so you may want to consider group travel as an alternative.

There are as many kinds of groups as there are travelers. Some people like being part of large tour groups, while others dislike being "herded" and prefer traveling with a small group. Look for tour companies that offer single accommodations, unless you don't mind sharing a room with someone you don't know. Some groups cover a lot of ground on their tours, while others concentrate on in-depth explorations of a smaller area. You may like to bicycle, walk, hike, or climb, and there are groups that specialize in these kinds of active vacations. If you prefer to see the sights from a bus or van, you can find groups for that too. Cultural tours, food and wine tours, archeological tours, history tours, art tours, battlefield tours—really, no matter what your passion, you can probably find a company that caters to it.

Companies like Road Scholar (formerly Elderhostel) offer small group tours designed especially for solo travelers that include a strong cultural/educational component. So does the Smithsonian Institution, the Archeological Conservancy, the Metropolitan Museum of Art, and several more. Use the internet to find companies that offer what you're looking for, and don't forget to look up reviews of their tours and service before you book with them.

Hitting the Road

So many of our clients tell us their dream is to buy a big RV and take off across the country to see it all at ground level and on their own schedules. I'm all for living your dream, but if you're considering buying a home on wheels, tap the brakes! The day you drive your brand-new RV off the lot, it starts losing value—and costing you significant money in maintenance. And it's not just caring for the RV, insuring it, and keeping it full of gas. If you're going to be away from home for a long period of time, you may have to put things in storage and get someone to keep the place up in your absence. All that's fine if you've foreseen these outlays and properly budgeted for them. But are you sure that ownership is really for you? How about, instead of taking the plunge, you stick a toe in the water first?

Renting an RV lets you enjoy the ride without saddling yourself with the big commitment. The costs are relatively low, and you can rent in most parts of the country and in Canada. Companies like Cruise America offer many kinds of discounts for long-term rentals, relocations, and seasonal specials. They'll even rent you the essential household items, so you don't have to pack more than you would for any other vacation. It's good to try before you buy because you come away with a clearer understanding of what kind of space you need, what traveling this way is like compared with hotel stays, and what the day-to-day costs are. You may find it's not your kind of thing at all, and that's a cheaper way to learn than suffering buyer's remorse.

Timeshares are another big buy that many people regret, because the rules on when and for how long you can use them can be very restrictive and they're not really "yours" in the way a vacation home would be. They're not cheap, and once you add up the costs involved, you might decide that staying in a short-term rental or a hotel is a better choice, with more flexibility and less expense. Getting rid of timeshares can be a big challenge, too, and they're notoriously hard to resell. I can count on one hand the number of clients I've had who were happy with their choice to buy into a timeshare.

Got a Quest?

Some of my favorite stories are about retirees who set out on epic trips on personal quests of one kind or another. One couple made it their business to visit every presidential birthplace across the United States. Others visit every national park, or the major battlefields of the American Civil War, or the Major League Baseball stadiums. One couple made the news by visiting every Costco! One of my clients loves the Olympics, so no matter where it's held, every four years she's at the Olympics. The possibilities are limited only by your imagination.

Learning Is Lifelong

We've talked a lot about travel and hobbies, but another way to keep yourself busy and your mind active is the pursuit of higher learning. If you enjoyed college but always wished you'd had time to learn more about a subject, you'll be happy to know that the opportunities to pursue those interests have never been better. You can take courses for credit or choose to audit them at most colleges and universities, and many have access to programs specifically for retirees. There are also all kinds of open-source sites online where you can "sit in" on courses at major universities around the world, including Harvard, Yale, and MIT.

Some retirees choose to advance their education in pursuit of a second career. One of our clients had worked in the oil industry for years, but as he neared retirement, he began to take foundational nursing courses, as he'd had experience working as a medic in the armed forces. By the time he retired, he didn't have far to go to become a licensed nurse, and now he works two or three days a week. Going back to school in his fifties was challenging, but he's very glad he did. He doesn't need the money, but it's deeply satisfying work for him.

Bottom Line

Retirement is what you make of it, so why not use this time to explore the world, try out new hobbies, and broaden your education? There are so many ways to make this chapter as rich and full of growth and excitement as any other time in your life—and now, you're the one calling the shots. Make the most of it!

CHAPTER 11

"Purpose—What Will My Life Mean?"

> *"What am I passionate about?"*
>
> *"Does anyone care what I have to say anymore?"*
>
> *"How do I find opportunities to volunteer and contribute to my community?"*

As the ad says, life comes at us fast. Most of us are so preoccupied during our working lives—juggling our jobs, family commitments, and our other responsibilities—that we have little or no time to consider the concept of what our legacy could be. But retirement grants us the gift of time in which to think and dream—and do. Too often when we're retired, we can feel sidelined, adrift, even irrelevant. But when we choose to give of ourselves or our wealth to make the world a better place, it can create a powerful sense of purpose, one that inspires us and leads us out of solitude and into community. Even in retirement, we need challenges and opportunities to do productive, meaningful work, because this keeps us vital and engaged. Making new friends around a common cause, applying what we know to philanthropic efforts, and interacting with the people we help all contribute to our mental health, sense of agency, and the legacy we'll leave behind in the hearts and minds of those whose lives we touch.

What does the word *legacy* mean to you? For some, it's a financial gift to found or fund a cause that matters to them. For others, it's improving the lives of one person or family at a time, using their special skills and talents. Some of us want our names on hospital wings; others merely want to be remembered as someone who helped where they could, who paid it forward to a less fortunate person in need. Maybe we just want to leave people with happy memories or to share our family stories and heritage with the next generation.

My client Charlie, a research chemist who plays the violin, had always dreamed of pursuing music as a profession. When he retired, he decided to form a string trio with a couple of friends who played viola and cello. They worked up a repertoire of show tunes, classical favorites, and even some rock songs and then took it on the road to nursing homes, schools, hospitals, and soup kitchens. They didn't charge a cent and made a lot of fans, brightening people's lives with the gift of music. Charlie wasn't thinking about legacy, but he's certainly leaving one simply by making people happy and spreading his joy in music. Most recently he played at his granddaughter's wedding, including for the bride's first dance—talk about making memories!

Another client, a physician, had worked at the top of his profession for many years, amassing an impressive net worth. He'd lost a child many years before, and when he retired, he honored her memory by sponsoring the complete renovation of the student health center where she'd gone to college and naming it after his daughter. He gave millions in her name to schools and organizations, creating a legacy of health and help for youth in both their names.

What will your legacy be? How do you want to be remembered? Most of us don't have the kinds of resources that building a college library or a cancer center require—but that doesn't mean we can't do something that will change lives for the better, including our own. There are many different approaches and levels of commitment to this kind of thing. Let's take a look at some of them, as you consider what might be right for you.

Taking Your Work to Retirement

Chances are, you've built a skill set in your years in the working world. Are there ways to take that skill set and share it with those who need it while keeping your skills sharp? Indeed there are, and opportunities abound in both paid and unpaid work.

Sometimes this looks pretty straightforward, as with dentists, doctors, and other medical professionals who volunteer to treat the poor and underserved. There are many programs that can connect you with patients who desperately need care they can't afford, both in the United States and abroad. These can be traveling clinics in specially equipped trucks that drive to various locations, where patients are treated. Some people do mission trips, taking their skills to where the need is greatest, and there are many organizations, both professional and charitable, putting these care teams together and getting them where they're needed.

Part-time work can both be financially rewarding and contribute to the public good. One of my clients is a very prominent oncologist who has officially retired but continues to work. She has no financial need at all, but she regularly travels to towns like Brownsville and

El Paso, Texas, because the local hospitals have a hard time finding doctors in her specialty. When they lose a doctor or a doctor goes on maternity leave, they're stuck, because they aren't typically the kinds of places that doctors will choose to live and practice. These locum positions let her mentor less-experienced doctors and provide an expert level of care to patients. She turns eighty this month and is still at it. At the end of the day, she finds tremendous satisfaction in the work, and knowing that she doesn't have to do it lets her enjoy it that much more.

Several of my clients have taken their knowledge and turned it into a new kind of opportunity by teaching in local schools. If you've spent your career amassing knowledge in the sciences, technology, or other fields and you have a hankering to share what you've learned with kids or motivated adult learners, consider checking out what kind of credential you'd need to become a classroom teacher. Again, you can make money doing this, but really, for most people it's about giving back. One retired history professor decided to return to the classroom by volunteering to teach incarcerated women at a prison.

A businessman client who loves golf found a way to take this passion to kids who otherwise might not have an opportunity to enjoy the game. He helped organize a charitable group whose mission was to teach golf to inner-city kids, and he was an enthusiastic participant as a teacher. He was able to use his business skills, too, in that he helped the organization get up and running with its 501C3 status and with fundraising.

In a world with so much need, those with special skills who aren't looking for paid work but simply to contribute are very much in demand. There are organizations that recruit plastic surgeons to repair cleft palates in developing countries and nurses who visit homeless shelters or teach childcare to new mothers. If you can do something—

really, nearly anything—in the healthcare arena, someone somewhere needs your help. And volunteering means you can do as little or as much as you feel you want to do.

One of my clients is a CPA who has found a second unpaid career in volunteering his skills. During tax time, he works with folks who come to him at the local public library for help with their tax forms, and he also serves on the board of that library as the treasurer. This helps him keep his skills fresh—those tax laws change every year, and CPAs need to do continuing education to keep up with them. And he provides meaningful service to people who otherwise would have a hard time doing their taxes as well as to the library and the patrons it serves in helping them stay afloat.

If you know how to hire, how to manage employees, how to run workshops, how to keep books, or how to write compelling prose for grant applications—all these are skill sets that nonprofits need badly. Look at your favorite local nonprofits and see if your knowledge and abilities are a match for their needs. Don't be afraid to make a call or send an email to the board president. Believe me, they'll be grateful to hear from you!

How Can Volunteering Help Me Stay Relevant?

We've talked a little about how some professions require continuing education to keep practitioners up to date and fully licensed. Certainly, this helps keep you relevant and abreast of the changes in your field and also makes you more valuable as a volunteer.

But there's more to staying in step with the world than keeping up with professional learning, and volunteering can also keep you current with other kinds of technology and information. If you volunteer for a group project, chances are that at least some of your meetings will be conducted online via Zoom or another video conference calling service. You may be tasked with creating and presenting informational talks, what we used to call slideshows, using the improved available technology to create high-quality graphics. You may get involved in projects that require you to master new software, like donor tracking or word processing. All these are great things to know in and of themselves, but they're also ways of staying on top of emerging technology and keeping your brain active and stimulated—and that's critical to your health and well-being.

The social stimulation you'll get from your new endeavor, the people you'll meet, and the fresh ideas and opinions you'll be exposed to will contribute to your well-being too. People of all ages and abilities coming together in a common cause create their own mini community of colleagues and coworkers. Meeting new people and getting to know them help us make our world grow rather than shrink through attrition. Shared goals give us a reason to keep moving forward rather than just watching life go by. And the sense of having done something meaningful helps us understand how our actions and involvement can have a positive impact on the lives we touch and make the world a better place. That's a powerful legacy in itself.

Other clients, often entrepreneurs with deep knowledge in their respective trades and businesses, make time to volunteer to mentor or advise young people working on their own start-ups. You can connect with potential mentees through local college and university programs, or you can volunteer with an organization like SCORE, which will put you together with folks looking for exactly your kind of expertise and arrange meetings for you with prospective mentees. This can lead to lasting and meaningful relationships and tremendous satisfaction in watching your mentee's venture grow and flourish with your help.

Working with Kids

If you love working with children and young people, there are many opportunities to do so. One woman we know volunteers to read aloud to a class of second graders and lead book discussions for them. Another, a retired art teacher, offers free craft classes to kids under the auspices of the local library.

There are opportunities to mentor kids who may lack positive role models in their communities or homes and whose lives can be changed for the better by having someone to talk to and spend time with. Organizations like Big Brother Big Sister Foundation make it easy to connect with a kid in need and will match you with a mentee. Another kind of opportunity is provided by groups like High Hopes Foundation, which need adult volunteers to help special needs or chronically ill children get the equipment and care they otherwise couldn't access. There are other groups who teach special needs kids to ride and care for horses or help young people learn animal husbandry, like 4-H.

Local shelters for homeless families or women's shelters that accommodate young kids always have wish lists of supplies, usually including clothing and toys, for parents and children experiencing hard times. And other groups specialize in finding permanent housing for families like these and furnishing their new homes with the essentials. There's really no greater gift for a family than to get out of the shelter system and into a permanent home, because it helps them escape the chaos of never being sure of where or if they'll eat or sleep and gives them a footing in a community.

Volunteers are usually welcomed by kids' sports teams and leagues, who are often short of coaches, equipment or field managers, or umpires and referees. If you love kids and sports, these kinds of volunteering opportunities give you a chance to support both.

We read recently of a retired man who volunteered to hold premature babies at a local hospital. Physical touch and comfort are so important for a newborn, and never more so than when they're ill or otherwise challenged. It gives him as much comfort as it gives them and is a beautiful and personal way to give.

If you're part of a faith community, consider volunteering to teach Sunday school. And if you'd like a part-time job that's important to child safety and will make you a hero to the kids you protect, consider becoming a crossing guard!

Mission Trips

If you belong to a faith community, chances are they offer opportunities to go on mission trips either in underserved areas in our country or abroad. The missions and countries differ, but generally you will be part of a team sent to address a specific need in a community, to build a school or a playground, dig a well, feed the hungry, or administer vaccines. Even if your skills aren't obviously suited to a particular mission, remember that there are always ancillary jobs that need to be filled with willing volunteers. Someone has to fill out intake paperwork, for instance, if you're traveling with a mobile clinic. Someone needs to account for equipment and supplies on a construction project; someone needs to cook or carry or do some other kind of less-skilled labor to free up those who are partnering on the work. Every job is important—vital, in fact—to the success of the mission trip, and you'll be a part of something worthwhile and life changing for those you're serving.

You can also find similar opportunities that are not connected to faith institutions. You don't have to be a master builder to work with Habitat for Humanity, for instance. They welcome anyone over age sixteen, with or without skills, to help on construction projects. Your contribution can be as simple as painting trim. They also operate retail stores that support their cause and always need people to help out there.

When You Want to Go Big

Some of us are fortunate enough to be able to do something that will positively impact many, many people even after we're gone. And while the scale of that philanthropy may vary, the impact we can make on individual lives makes all the difference to those you help.

One man we know of began laying the foundation of the fortune he made when he was in his twenties, buying and rehabbing homes as a way to build wealth. He rose to tremendous success and prominence in a different area of the housing business but never lost a personal interest in creating livable, comfortable homes from what were nearly teardowns. When he began edging toward retirement, he began thinking in terms of what he wanted to leave behind. There was plenty of money to gift his children and grandchildren; his wife would be provided for in the event of his death. He realized that near the area where he'd grown up, there were whole neighborhoods hollowed out by urban blight and many potential homes that could house the unhoused if they were renovated. He founded a charity to do exactly that—to purchase and fix up homes and to reclaim neighborhoods in the process. Every house represents a fresh start for a family in need, and creating this organization and overseeing the work it does has given him tremendous purpose and joy.

Our wealthier clients often express a desire to make an impactful gift to their communities or to those in need, and we're able to help them set up the financial planning to increase their gifts using tax strategies that make sure more of their money gets to the people who need it and not the IRS. One couple had committed to multiple contributions to three universities and was planning on simply writing them checks. When they came to us for advice, we modeled different tax years, what their needs and income were likely to be, and looked at the total amount they were going to give. It was quite a bit of work, but we were able to identify the ideal year to make that gift. They took that information and went to the planned giving groups at these three different colleges to let them know what they wanted to do and how theirs was going to be a multiyear gift. That planning allowed much more of their gifts to go to the intended recipients rather than the IRS.

Be Careful Not to Overcommit

When you begin volunteering, it's all too easy to be talked into taking on more than you really can do and spreading yourself too thin. That can lead to burnout, resentment, and ultimately to pulling away from your commitments. Instead, start small. Offer a set number of hours a week or month and stick to it. See how you and the charity you've chosen work together. There will always be more demand than there are people to fill these volunteer jobs, so if you and a particular cause don't feel like the right fit, try something else. It's easier to decide to commit more time than to take your time back from an organization that needs your help. You can feel guilty and then end up with a commitment that feels more like a job than retirement endeavor.

Bottom Line

When we talk about leaving a legacy, it doesn't have to be expressed as financial support. Devote your gifts, talents, and enthusiasm to giving back. Consider volunteering in your community or anywhere you see a need. Seek out opportunities to learn new technology and to meet new people. And don't forget to save time for yourself to enjoy your retirement your way!

AFTERWORD

Retirement is one of the most significant transitions in life—a chance to pause, reflect, and build something new. It is both a financial puzzle and a deeply personal journey, one that blends the practical with the emotional. As we've explored throughout this book, creating a successful retirement is about more than just numbers on a spreadsheet. It's about designing a life that excites you, challenges you, and gives you purpose.

The first step is building a solid foundation. Understanding your finances—your income, investments, and tax strategy—is essential. The peace of mind that comes from knowing your financial house is in order allows you to confidently take the leap into this next phase. Whether it is deciding when to retire, deciding how to take distributions, or crafting a strategy for leaving a legacy, the "nuts and bolts" of retirement are your safety net.

But financial security is only one piece of the puzzle. What comes next is where the real magic happens. This next chapter of your life is about redefining your identity, nurturing relationships, and discovering what truly brings you joy. Retirement gives you the freedom to reinvent yourself, to try new things, to give back, and to deepen the connections that matter most. It is an opportunity to live not just with intention but with curiosity and courage.

As you move forward, remember that it's okay to have doubts. It's okay to not have everything figured out right away. Just as you adjusted to life's many transitions before this one, you'll find your rhythm here too. Build routines that fulfill you. Lean into your passions. Seek out communities that energize you. This chapter is yours to write, and it can be as rich and colorful as you want it to be.

Ultimately, retirement isn't about what you leave behind. It's about what you're stepping into—more time for the people and passions you love, new challenges that bring excitement and growth, and a life that reflects everything you've worked so hard to build.

So, take a deep breath, look ahead, and trust that you've prepared for this moment in every way.

Go build a life you love.

www.ingramcontent.com/pod-product-compliance
Lightning Source LLC
La Vergne TN
LVHW091548040926
847245LV00001B/6